APPLICATIONS OF GRAM

Developing Communication Skills

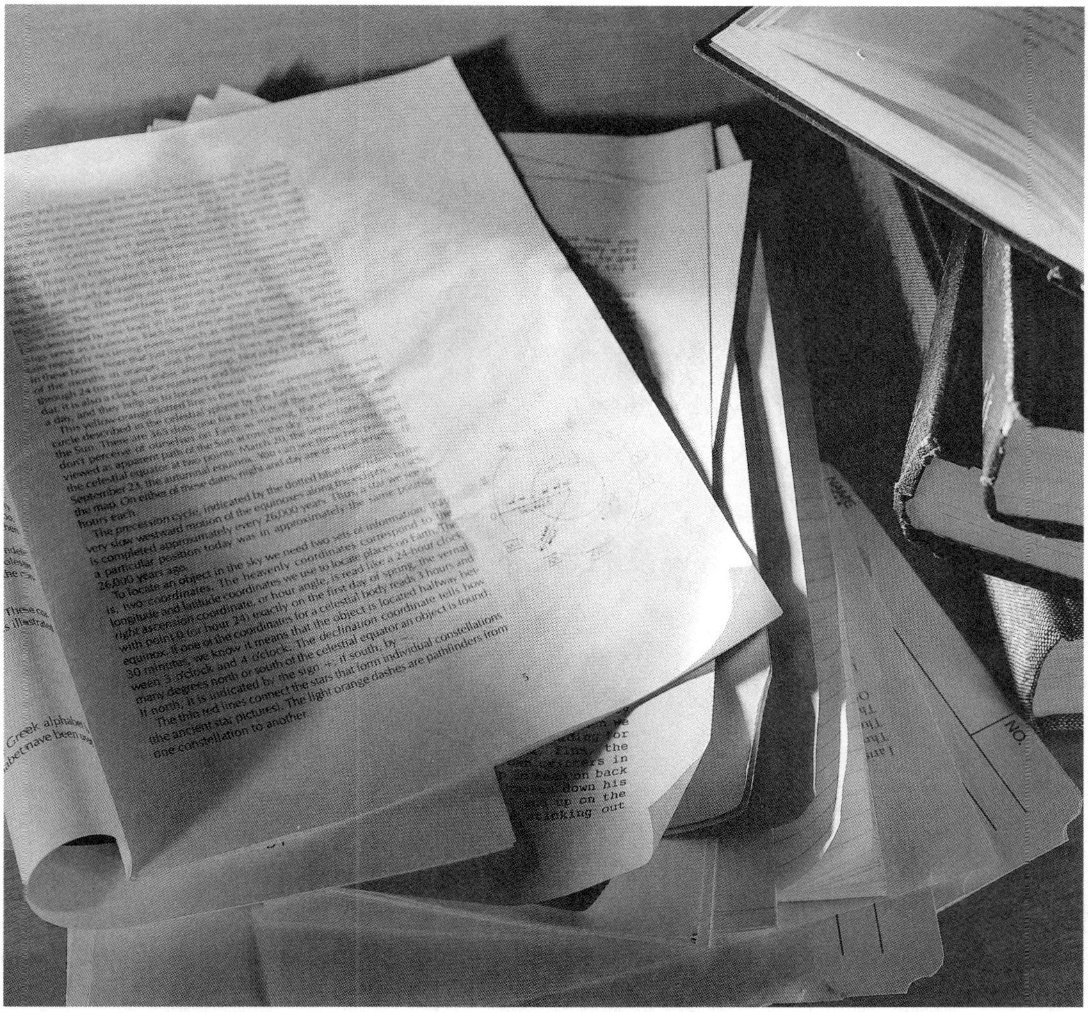

Christian Liberty Press Arlington Heights, Illinois

A publication of

Christian Liberty Press

502 West Euclid Avenue

Arlington Heights, Illinois 60004

www.christianlibertypress.com

Scripture references are conformed to The Holy Bible, New King James Version ©1982, Thomas Nelson, Inc., so that modern readers may gain greater comprehension of the Word of God.

Sloan, Annie Lee, revised and edited by Garry J. Moes

APPLICATIONS OF GRAMMAR, BOOK 5

DEVELOPING COMMUNICATION SKILLS

Includes glossary and index

1. English Language—Grammar and Composition

Copyediting by Diane C. Olson

Layout by Edward J. Shewan

ISBN 978–1-930367-31-9
        1-930367-31-7

Printed in the United States of America

Preface

This book is intended to lay a proper foundation for the student's effectiveness in communicating with the English language. The student will learn the basics of English grammar, including the definition and usage of verbs, nouns, adjectives, adverbs, and other parts of speech. In addition, the student will examine how these are to be properly used in phrases, clauses, sentences, paragraphs, and composition. The *Applications of Grammar* series is designed to develop students' skills in using the rules of grammar to communicate effectively for the glory of God.

While some today would discard the need for grammar, this text affirms that the learning of grammatical rules and their proper usage is foundational to good communication. The distinctions between words, their relation to each other in a sentence, and the rules that govern language are the basic building blocks of writing well.

This text is designed to be read carefully by the student so that he may review the grammar knowledge he has already learned and build upon it with new writing skills. Each lesson should be read carefully and reviewed as necessary. Some of the words used in the text may be new to the student's vocabulary, and their spelling unfamiliar. Therefore, a glossary and index are located at the back of this volume to provide students and teachers with additional reference material.

Many of the lessons will require use of a dictionary. While an unabridged dictionary would be useful, a standard, full-sized, collegiate-level dictionary will be more useful. Small, pocket-size, or greatly abridged desktop editions will likely not provide the amount of information that the student will need to complete many of the lessons in this book. It would also be helpful if the student had access to a set of encyclopedias or other reference works. These will be useful in the several writing assignments included in this textbook. If your school or home does not have adequate resources of this nature, you should visit your local library.

THE AUTHOR

Mrs. Annie Lee Sloan earned her B.S. and M.S. degrees at East Texas State University and did postgraduate work at the University of Alabama, Tuscaloosa. She has taught in elementary and junior high schools for many years. Mrs. Sloan has also taught communication skills at Harry M. Ayers State Technical College in Anniston, Alabama.

THE EDITOR

Garry J. Moes is a freelance writer, textbook author, and communications consult from Murphys, California. He earned his bachelor of arts degree in journalism from Michigan State University, East Lansing, Michigan, and did his postgraduate research at Scandinavian Christian University's Nordic College of Journalism in Sweden. He was a writer, reporter, and editor for the Associated Press for twenty-one years and has been an essayist, international correspondent, and executive editor for several Christian periodicals.

Table of Contents

ACKNOWLEDGMENTS

The author wishes to give credit to the following sources from which facts were taken for this series and from which written permission has been granted to use these facts.

Anniston Star, The, Joe Distelheim, exec. ed. (P.O. Box 189, Anniston, AL 36202).

Compton's Encyclopedia. (Chicago: Compton's Learning Company).

National Parkways, E.R. Randell, ed. (Casper, WY: World-Wide Research and Publishing Company).

The following were consulted on grammatical topics during revision and editing:

Associated Press Stylebook and Libel Manual, The, revised edition, Christopher W. French, ed. (Reading, MA: Addison-Wesley Publishing Company, Inc., 1987).

Chapman, James A., *Handbook of Grammar and Composition*, 2nd ed., revised. (Pensacola, FL: A Beka Book Publications, 1985).

Fowler, H. W., *A Dictionary of Modern English Usage*, 2nd ed., revised and edited by Sir Ernest Gowers. (Oxford: Oxford University Press, 1985).

Kierzek, John M., and Walker Gibson, *The Macmillan Handbook of English*, 6th ed., revised by Robert F. Willson, Jr. (New York: Macmillan Publishing Co., Inc., 1977).

Leslie, Louis A., *20,000 Words*, 7th ed. (New York: McGraw-Hill Book Company,1977).

Webster, Noah, *American Dictionary of the English Language*, facsimile 1st ed., 1828, 5th ed. (San Francisco: Foundation for American Christian Education, 1987).

Webster's II New Riverside Dictionary. (New York: The Berkley Publishing Group, copyright 1984, Houghton Mifflin Company).

Webster's Third New International Dictionary, unabridged, Philip Babcock Gove, sen. ed. (Springfield, MA: Merriam-Webster Inc., Publishers, 1986).

Wykoff, George S., and Harry Shaw, *The Harper Handbook of College Composition*, 2nd ed. (New York: Harper & Brothers, Publishers, 1957).

Introduction

THE CHRISTIAN VIEW OF LANGUAGE

Students often wonder why they have to study grammar and composition when they already know how to talk and write. Although basic communication skills may be evident, every student needs to thoroughly learn not only how language works but how to use it accurately. In order to speak and write well, students must acquire a proper understanding of grammatical definitions, functions, structures, and rules so that they may verbalize their thoughts with clarity and precision. Few skills are more important to Christian students than the ability to effectively communicate through the written and spoken word.

The student will be able to study language more purposefully if he begins with an understanding of the Christian view of language. Sadly, some students merely study language and grammar because they have been made to do so. They fail to grasp that, because we are made in God's image, good communication is essential to our service to God. As an image bearer of God, the student should consider how the Bible can direct his study of language. Through faith in Jesus Christ he can be reconciled to God and learn how to use language to the end for which it was created. Because language did not originate with us, we do not have the right to use it any way we wish. We must be guided by the Bible. Language skills are not neutral; they must be oriented toward reading, writing, and speaking the truth in love. Linguistic abilities should be developed as part of the student's chief end to glorify God and enjoy Him forever.

GOD IS THE ORIGIN OF LANGUAGE

> In the beginning God created the heaven and the earth. And the earth was without form and void; and darkness was upon the face of the deep. And the Spirit of God moved over the face of the waters. And God *said* ... (Genesis 1:1–3).

God is the origin of language, for the three persons of the Trinity spoke to each other before time began. When the Father, the Son, and the Holy Spirit speak to each other eternally, their communication is perfect; there is never one word of misunderstanding! The Son of God is called the *Word* of God, and the Holy Spirit searches the mind of God and communicates with spiritual words (1 Corinthians 2:10–13). When God created the heavens and the earth, He spoke it into existence by the Word of His power. When He spoke, He uttered a series of sounds—audible symbols that communicated His meaning and brought the creation into being. When God spoke, His Word conveyed both infinite power and eternal meaning—*infinite power* because He manifested His absolute will, and *eternal meaning* because He expressed His infinite mind. His infinite wisdom is revealed in creation, and the creatures He has made serve the purpose of communicating His glory. Thus the rock, for example, is used as a picture of God's unchanging character. Creation itself was designed to provide the basic terms and environment for language.

GOD GAVE MAN THE GIFT OF LANGUAGE

When God created man in His own image, He gave him the gift of language—the ability to communicate with words. He gave man the ability, like Himself, to convey meaning with his words, but He did not impart the infinite creative power of His speech. Thus, God's Word is the final authority, and men are to speak in submission to that Word. The language of man is to be subject to God, for man by his speech has no power to create or change what God has made. Yet there is a great power to human speech. It not only sets on fire the course of our lives but the course of history as well (James 3:6).

Because language is a gift of God, it has a purpose. It was given first of all as the means by which God would communicate to man. As such, it has a high and holy place in our lives. From the beginning God chose to communicate with man. The first words spoken to Adam and Eve were His charge, "Be fruitful, and multiply, and replenish the earth ..." (Genesis 1:28). God's desire to communicate with Adam and Eve in the Garden of Eden was central to their fellowship. They "heard the voice of the Lord God walking in the cool of the day..." (Genesis 3:8). Secondly, language was given so that man would respond to God. God created mankind to praise His name and answer His call. Thirdly, it was given for men to communicate with each other in subjection to God's word. People were given the ability to talk to one another and thereby develop marriage, the family, and other social relationships. The primary instrument for building these relationships is verbal communication. God's purpose for language should direct our study of it.

RULES FOR COMMUNICATION

For many students, rules are a burden to be disregarded. But the student who is willing to submit to God's order will seek to develop precision in communicating. Because God is a God of order and truth, He has demonstrated the proper use of language in His speech from the dawn of history. For people to communicate properly and effectively with one another, God not only gave language but with it the basic principles of good communication. This does not mean that we have a divinely revealed set of rules from God, but we can learn from the Bible's use of language and build upon the principles that have been learned in the past. In particular, the Bible and the Christian religion have had a central role in molding the English language.

Consequently, the study of grammar—the body of rules for speaking and writing—should be based on the fact that God is the Creator of language and thereby the Originator of its order. Good grammar reflects His logic and manifests the orderly structure of His mind. By learning the rules of proper usage, the student will know how to make his thoughts known and communicate in a compelling manner. His purpose is not simply to be able to communicate, however, but to use language effectively to communicate God's truth.

Language and grammar are not mere human conventions that spring from chance evolution to fill a human need. Language expresses a people's culture, religion, and history. This is why language changes over time. Each language has its own characteristics and rules of usage. But every language displays an underlying unity with other languages. Every language is a verbal system of communication. Each has similar patterns of grammar, though not expressed in exactly the same way. Yet at bottom, the basic principles of grammatical structure are common to every language, which is why writings from one language can be translated into another. While the basic principles of grammar may be adapted in unique ways, these are derived from the original language given by God to man.

LANGUAGE CORRUPTED BY SIN

After our first parents sinned, the same Voice that spoke the world into existence now stood in judgment over mankind. And the language that had been given as a gift to man by the Father of Truth had now been distorted by the Father of Lies. That which was created to praise and worship God had now been used to rebel against the Author of language. Man's fellowship with the Living God had been broken, and he no longer desired to hear Him speak.

In addition, the Bible tells us that after the Great Flood, men united by a common language sought unity apart from God at the Tower of Babel. Seeing this, God confused their one language by dividing it into many and scattered them over the face of the whole earth. Language was thus changed by God to keep men from disobeying His mandate. Because of these different languages, there are now barriers between men when they communicate; and sin has continued to pervert the use of language, making it an instrument of lies and manipulation. Today, there are those who would reject all form and grammar and seek to justify any use of language and any breaking of the rules of grammar. As a result, confusion reigns in many quarters, and many people have great difficulty clearly articulating their thoughts in speech and writing.

THE RESTORATION OF LANGUAGE IN JESUS CHRIST

God chose to restore language in His Son. Jesus, as the second Adam, was sent into the world to undo the sin of the first Adam and its consequences (Romans 5:19). Jesus, who is the Word, was with God in the creation because He is God (John 1:1–3). Jesus is the *logos* or revelation of God to man, for God has spoken to us in His Son (Hebrews 1:1, 2). There is no other name under heaven given among men, whereby we must be saved (Acts 4:12). God's will to communicate with man was one factor that motivated Him to restore language to its rightful state in Christ Jesus. By His death and resurrection, Christ not only provides forgiveness of sin, but also newness of life to those who receive Him by faith. As the Truth, Christ calls His disciples to speak the oracles of God (1 Peter 4:11), lay aside lies, and speak truth to one another (Ephesians 4:25). Jesus is the true source of the meaning of all things. He declared, "'I am the Alpha and Omega, the Beginning and the End,' says the Lord, 'who is and who was and who is to come, the Almighty'" (Rev. 1:8). As R. J. Rushdoony states:

> Christ's statement has reshaped Western languages and grammars, and, through Bible translation, is reshaping the languages of peoples all over the world. Bible translation is an exacting task, because it involves in effect the reworking of a language in order to make it carry the meaning of the Bible. This means a new view of the world, of God, time and language.... Our ideas of grammar, of tense, syntax, and structure, of thought and meaning, bear a Christian imprint.[1]

Students who profess the Christian faith should have a unique appreciation of the role of verbal communication. It is the Christian, above all, who should seek to be clear and accurate in his use of the written word. His God-given duty is to use language with integrity and accuracy for the sake of promoting the gospel and Kingdom of Jesus Christ. Noah Webster saw this in his day when he wrote:

> If the language can be improved in regularity, so as to be more easily acquired by our own citizens, and by foreigners, and thus be rendered a more useful instrument for

---

1. Rousas J. Rushdoony, *The Philosophy of the Christian Curriculum* (Vallecito, CA: Ross House Books, 1985), p. 49–50.

the propagation of science, arts, civilization and Christianity; if it can be rescued from the mischievous influence of ...that dabbling spirit of innovation which is perpetually disturbing its settled usages and filling it with anomalies; if, in short, our vernacular language can be redeemed from corruptions, and...our literature from degradation; it would be a source of great satisfaction to me to be one among the instruments of promoting these valuable objects.[2]

To show that the Christian has the marvelous opportunity to employ language and its power for the service of the gospel, Gary DeMar asserts:

Ideas put to paper and acted upon with the highest energy and uncompromising zeal can change the world. Even the worst ideas have been used for this very purpose. If minds are going to be transformed and civilizations changed, then Christians must learn to write and write well. Writing is a sword, mightier than all the weapons of war because writing carries with it ideas that penetrate deeper than any bullet. Writing about the right things in the right way can serve as an antidote to the writings of skepticism and tyranny that have plundered the hearts and minds of generations of desperate people around the world....[3]

Language as the gift of God needs to be cultivated for serving God. It will not only help the student in academic studies, but in every area of communication, at home, at church, and on the job. Proper English skills are a great asset in serving Christ effectively in one's calling. The student's skill in using English will make a good first impression when he sits for an interview and as he labors in the workplace. The student should take advantage of the time and opportunity he now has available to develop proficiency in English communication. May God bless you as you seek to glorify Him, not only by learning the proper use of English, but in using God's gift of language to spread His Word to every nation.

---

2.   Noah Webster, *An American Dictionary of the English Language* (New York, NY: S. Converse, 1828); reprint by (San Francisco, CA: Foundation for American Christian Education, 1987), preface.

3.   Gary DeMar, *Surviving College Successfully* (Brentwood, TN: Wolgemuth & Hyatt Publishers, Inc., 1988), p.225.

Developing Communication Skills

Lesson One

◆ *Paragraphs*

A **paragraph** is *a group of sentences*, all of which tell about the same **topic**. Every paragraph has one basic sentence called the *topic sentence*, which has two principal parts: the *topic* and the *clew*. The **topic** is definite and specific; whereas, the **clew** is general enough to give the writer room for explanations and information developing the topic.

Example: *Religion is a necessary, an indispensable element in any great human character.* There is no living without it. Religion is the tie that connects man to his Creator, and holds him to his throne.   (Daniel Webster, 1782–1852)

In the paragraph above, the first sentence (italicized) is the topic sentence, stating the main theme or idea of the paragraph. Within the topic sentence *religion* is the specific or definite topic, and the rest of the sentence contains the general clew. This topic sentence tells us that all of the remaining sentences in the paragraph should deal with the subject of religion and should tell us how religion is a necessary part of human greatness. When we examine the other two sentences in this paragraph, we see that both of them indeed deal with religion and give us additional information on how religion is indispensable.

The *topic sentence* is a guide to both the writer and the reader. It helps the writer to remain focused on his subject and to avoid introducing irrelevant material that may confuse the reader or distract from the writer's point. A good topic sentence helps the reader follow the logical progression of the writer's thoughts.

Although simple sentences are perhaps the clearest and most effective types of topic sentences, a good writer will use a variety of topic sentences if his work extends for several paragraphs. Topics may be stated in phrases or in clauses of compound, complex, or compound-complex sentences. Topic sentences may be declarative, interrogatory, exclamatory, or imperative. (*See Glossary for definitions of these terms.*)

Paragraphs can generally be classified in one of four categories:

1. *Expository* paragraphs *explain* a topic.

2. *Narrative* paragraphs *tell* a story.

3. *Descriptive* paragraphs *describe* a topic.

4. *Argumentative* paragraphs make a statement and try to prove it to be true.

1

To review what you have learned about paragraphs in this lesson, complete the following:

A paragraph is a _____ of sentences, all of which tell about the same _____. A paragraph has one basic sentence called the _____ sentence, which has two principal parts: the _____ and the _____. The _____ is definite and specific; whereas, the _____ is general enough to give the writer room for explanations and information to _____ the topic.

Expository paragraphs _____.

Narrative paragraphs _____.

Descriptive paragraphs _____.

Argumentative paragraphs _____.

Lesson Two

◆ *Narrative Paragraph*

Write a ***narrative paragraph*** about an experience that you had during the summer. Choose your topic carefully so that your teacher can easily identify both your topic and your clew. Then be sure that all you write fits both. Remember that narrative writing *tells a story.* It answers the questions: *What happened? How did it happen? When did it happen? Where did it happen? Who was involved?*

_____

_____

_____

_____

_____

_____

_____

_____

_____

_____

_____

_____

_____

_____

Lesson Three

◆ *Spelling*

Learn to pronounce and spell the following words.

1. singular	7. prepositional	13. refrigerator
2. pictorial	8. determined	14. recognition
3. expository	9. compound	15. respectfully
4. narrative	10. collective	16. advancement
5. descriptive	11. concrete	17. exploration
6. argumentative	12. independence	18. representation

Lesson Four

◆ *Spelling and Vocabulary*

Learn to pronounce, spell, and identify the following words.

1. antecedent	6. companionship	11. mascot
2. eroded	7. originality	12. obscured
3. diseased	8. immunized	13. symbolic
4. abstract	9. initially	14. deteriorate
5. designate	10. technology	

Lesson Five

◆ *Vocabulary*

Write the words from *Lesson 4* beside their definitions in the following.

1. Fellowship among friends   _____

2. Substituting abstract representations for concrete objects   _____

3. A noun or pronoun to which another pronoun refers   _____

4. Become inferior in quality or value   _____

5. Expressed without reference to a specific instance or object   _____

6. Person, animal, or object adopted by a group as a symbol   _____

7. Worn away   _____

8. Newness or freshness in design, style, or idea   _____

9. The application of scientific knowledge, especially in industry   _____

10. Sickly; lacking health or soundness, disordered   _____

11. Protected against disease   _____

12. Not clearly seen   _____

13. To point out, characterize, appoint, or select   _____

14. At first   _____

Lesson Six

◆ *Classification of Nouns*

Nouns are words that name *persons, places, things, qualities, actions,* or *ideas.* Nouns are classified as *common* or *proper.* **Common nouns** refer to the general names of people, places, things, qualities, actions, or ideas. **Proper nouns** refer to specific names of members of these groupings. Proper nouns always begin with a *capital letter.*

Examples:

	Common Nouns	Proper Nouns
Person:	neighbor	Sally
Place:	school	Central Christian High School
Thing:	refrigerator	General Electric
Idea:	religion	Christianity
Quality:	ethnicity	Jewishness
Action:	division	Balkanization

Write lists of common nouns and some proper nouns that might be related to them.

People

Common Nouns   *Proper Nouns*

1. _____   _____

2. _____   _____

3. _____   _____

4. _____   _____

5. _____   _____

Places

Common Nouns   *Proper Nouns*

1. _____   _____

2. _____   _____

3. _____   _____

4. _____   _____

5. _____   _____

Things

Common Nouns   **Proper Nouns**

1. _____   _____

2. _____   _____

3. _____   _____

4. _____   _____

5. _____   _____

Ideas, Qualities, or Actions

Common Nouns   **Proper Nouns**

1. _____   _____

2. _____   _____

3. _____   _____

4. _____   _____

5. _____   _____

Lesson Seven

◆ *Compound and Concrete Nouns*

Nouns, both common and proper, may also be classified as *compound, concrete, collective,* or *abstract*. In this lesson, we will consider *compound* and *concrete* nouns.

Compound nouns consist of two or more words joined into a single noun. The parts of some compound nouns may be joined by hyphens. Others, often proper nouns, consist of two words **not** connected by hyphens.

Examples: *bookcase, sister-in-law, Bay Area*

Make a list of some *compound nouns*.

Joined   **Hyphenated**   **Two-word**

_____   _____   _____

_____   _____   _____

_____   _____   _____

_____   _____   _____

_____   _____   _____

Concrete nouns are words that name objects that can be perceived by the senses of touch, sight, taste, hearing, or smell.

Examples: *wind, animal, milk, laughter, smoke*

Make a list of some concrete nouns.

Sight	Hearing	Touch	Taste	Smell
_____	_____	_____	_____	_____
_____	_____	_____	_____	_____
_____	_____	_____	_____	_____
_____	_____	_____	_____	_____
_____	_____	_____	_____	_____

Lesson Eight

◆ Abstract and Collective Nouns

Abstract nouns are words naming concepts that cannot be perceived by the senses. Generally, they name *ideas* or *qualities*. Complete the following list with additional *abstract nouns*.

1. *kindness*
2. *companionship*
3. *leadership*
4. *management*
5. *originality*
6. _____
7. _____
8. _____
9. _____
10. _____
11. _____
12. _____
13. _____
14. _____
15. _____

Collective nouns refer to groups considered as units. They may name *people, places, things, ideas, qualities,* or *actions.* Complete the following list with additional collective nouns.

1. *assembly*
2. *band*
3. *collection*
4. *news*
5. _____
6. _____
7. _____
8. _____
9. _____
10. _____
11. _____
12. _____

Lesson Nine

◆ Subject and Verb Agreement

Verbs must agree with their subjects in *number* and *person*. The term **number** refers to whether a noun is *singular* or *plural*. The term **person** usually refers to *pronouns* and indicates whether the subject is the one speaking (*first person*), the one spoken to (*second person*), or the one spoken about (*third person*).

In this lesson and the next one, we will be concerned with *agreement in number* between subjects and verbs. If the subject is singular, the verb must also be _____. If the subject is plural, the verb must also be _____.

Confusion often arises when a subject of a certain number is followed by a prepositional phrase containing a noun or pronoun of another number. Generally, prepositional phrases following a subject do not affect the number of the subject.

Examples: 1.   The *horses* in the pasture *were grazing* contentedly.

2.   The *corn* in the fields *was* still green.

Sometimes, however, the object of the preposition in a prepositional phrase following a subject is the antecedent of an *indefinite-pronoun subject.* The antecedent in the prepositional phrase then determines the number of the subject and verb, since pronouns must agree with their antecedents in number, just as subjects and verbs must agree in number.

Examples: 1.   *Some* of the **vegetables** *are* ruined.

Some of the **water** *is* dirty.

2.   *One third* of the **land** *is* badly eroded.

One third of the **trees** *are* diseased.

From the examples above, you can see that if the subject is an indefinite pronoun or a fraction, its number is determined by its antecedent (in bold type above), which, in these examples, is the object of the preposition following the subject.

As a general rule, nouns ending with *s* are *plural*, while action verbs ending with *s* are *singular* in *number, present tense,* and in the *third person.*

Examples: 1.   The *rain* (singular subject) in our area *continues* (singular verb) to come.

2.   Those *musicians* (plural subject) *amaze* (plural verb) me with their skill.

Below each of the following sentences, write the subject, the correct verb, and the number of the subject-verb construction.

1.   The bridge connecting the islands (has, have) been closed.

   subject _____   *verb* _____   *number* _____

2.   More than half of the citizens (was, were) opposed to the project.

   subject _____   *verb* _____   *number* _____

3.   Some of them (has, have) always wanted to stay home on holidays.

   subject _____   *verb* _____   *number* _____

4.   One of the doctors' chief objections (has, have) been a fear of the spread of disease.

   subject _____   *verb* _____   *number* _____

5. The first transaction between the two companies (was, were) made two years ago.

    subject _____   *verb* _____   *number* _____

6. The company overseeing the project (was, were) called Microtech.

    subject _____   *verb* _____   *number* _____

7. Advancements in technology (continue, continues) to amaze us.

    subject _____   *verb* _____   *number* _____

8. His exploits often (takes, take) us by surprise.

    subject _____   *verb* _____   *number* _____

9. Not all funds spent on research (proves, prove) to be a wise investment.

    subject _____   *verb* _____   *number* _____

10. Most of the money (goes, go) for salaries.

    subject _____   *verb* _____   *number* _____

11. A few of the projects (becomes, become) sources of solutions to troubling problems.

    subject _____   *verb* _____   *number* _____

12. Some of the benefits (does, do) eventually reach the people who need them.

    subject _____   *verb* _____   *number* _____

Lesson Ten

◆ *Subjects Connected with 'and'*

I. Subjects in series or subjects connected by the coordinating conjunction *and* are called **compound subjects**. Compound subjects generally require a plural verb, regardless of whether the subjects are singular or plural nouns or pronouns individually.

Examples: 1. *Boys and girls* **have** *different interests.*

                2. *Books, pencils, and paper* **are** *essential tools of every student.*

II. There are *four exceptions* to the above rule:

    1. Compound subjects preceded by the word *each*.

    2. Compound subjects preceded by the word *every*.

    3. Compound subjects that refer to *one person*.

    4. Compound subjects that refer to a *single thing* or *unit*.

Examples: 1. *Each man, woman, and child **receives** proper recognition in our church.*

2. *Every dog and cat in the county **is expected** to be immunized.*

3. The *secretary and receptionist **represents** her employer well.*

4. *Bread and water **was** the prisoner's only meal.*

III. Three rules must be remembered when using the ***correlative conjunctions*** *either...or* and *neither...nor* to connect compound subjects.

1. If both subjects are singular, the verb must be singular.

2. If both subjects are plural, the verb must be plural.

3. If one subject is singular and one is plural, the subject closer to the verb in the sentence determines the number of the verb. (This same rule applies to compound subjects joined by the coordinating conjunctions *or* and *nor*.)

Examples: 1. *Either rain or snow **adds** moisture to the soil.*

2. *Neither our coaches nor our teachers **have** ever lived on a farm.*

3. *Either my brother or my parents **feed** the horses each morning.*

IV. When *either* or *neither* is used as an **adjective** preceding a subject, the subject is always singular and requires a singular verb.

Examples: 1. *Either boy **qualifies** for the prize.*

2. *Neither girl **shows** any sign of fatigue.*

V. When *either* or *neither* is a *pronoun* used as a subject, it is always singular and requires a singular verb.

Examples: 1. *Neither **fits** my budget.*

2. *Either **suits** my taste in dresses.*

VI. Choosing the correct verb to agree with its subject in a *question* (interrogatory sentence) requires looking ahead in the sentence to determine the number of the subject, since subjects generally follow verbs in questions.

Examples: 1. *Doesn't anyone listen to me anymore?*

2. *Aren't the rules for the game more explicit than that?*

Below the following sentences, write the subject, the correct verb, and the number.

1. Those cookies (has, have) lost their crispness.

   subject _____   verb _____   number _____

2. Every cow, horse, and sheep on the farm (was, were) exposed to the disease.

   subject _____   verb _____   number _____

3. Either his courage or his skill (carries, carry) him to further accomplishments.

   subject _____   verb _____   number _____

4. Half of my friends (lives, live) in my neighborhood.

   subject _____   verb _____   number _____

5. Each of the visitors always (shows, show) a different interest in the displays.

   subject _____   verb _____   number _____

6. Neither the lawyer nor the judge (seems, seem) to understand her case.

   subject _____   verb _____   number _____

7. (Doesn't, Don't) either team have a mascot?

   subject _____   verb _____   number _____

8. Half of the fruit (spoils, spoil) before reaching the market.

   subject _____   verb _____   number _____

9. Every one of her children (admires, admire) her faithfulness to them.

   subject _____   verb _____   number _____

10. (Is, Are) neither of the appliances American-made?

    subject _____   verb _____   number _____

11. The owner and manager of the shop (treats, treat) all of his customers respectfully.

    subject _____   verb _____   number _____

12. Peaches and ice cream (makes, make) a refreshing dessert.

    subject _____   verb _____   number _____

13. Neither the cost for the supplies nor the charges for labor (amounts, amount) to more than we expected.

     subject _____   *verb* _____   *number* _____

14. Either the tomatoes or the oranges (gives, give) us vitamin C.

     subject _____   *verb* _____   *number* _____

15. All of the market value of some antiques (is, are) often obscured by bidding.

     subject _____   *verb* _____   *number* _____

Lesson Eleven

◆ *Spelling*

Learn to pronounce and spell the following words.

1. positively	7. availability	13. destructiveness
2. negatively	8. industrial	14. sufficiently
3. photographers	9. California	15. responsibilities
4. productivity	10. acreage	16. immeasurable
5. negligent	11. preservation	17. parenthetic
6. annually	12. phenomena	18. interrupter

Lesson Twelve

◆ *Spelling and Vocabulary*

Learn to pronounce, spell, and identify the following words.

1. substantive	6. potential	11. prolific
2. extinction	7. concession	12. precision
3. dissolution	8. encroachment	13. diverse
4. demographic	9. orchard	14. incubation
5. visionary	10. computations	

Lesson Thirteen

◆ *Vocabulary*

Each of the words in *Lesson 12* will fit in one of the following sentences to make the sentence complete. Write the words where they fit.

1. The time between exposure to a disease and its appearance is the _____ period.

2. Skills needed for basketball are _____ from those needed for tennis.

3. The _____ with which this watch is made accounts for its high cost.

4. Our _____ was full of fruit and nut trees.

5. Her mathematical _____ proved to be accurate.

6. The gradual _____ of the sea upon the shore washed away much of the beach.

7. High production figures indicated the orchard trees were more _____ than usual.

8. The _____ of the Communist governments in Eastern Europe began suddenly during the late 1980s.

9. His message was more _____ than entertaining.

10. His _____ research indicated a significant movement of people from the West Coast into the Rocky Mountain area during the past decade.

11. The _____ for an earthquake in Southern California is always present.

12. The negotiators sought to extract a _____ from each side in the dispute in order to move the talks toward conclusion.

13. The proposals for new advances in space exploration seem quite _____.

14. Without constant protection of some species of animals and plants, several might face _____.

Lesson Fourteen

◆ *Expository Paragraph*

Write an *expository paragraph* in which you explain how you did some project that was your responsibility during the summer months or past school year. If you did not have such a project to complete, select a hypothetical project and explain how it could be carried out. Choose your *topic sentence* carefully so that your teacher will know exactly what your project was and what facts you will attempt to develop in explaining it. You might answer the questions *when?*, *where?*, *why?*, and *how?* in your paragraph.

Lesson Fifteen

◆ *Subject-Verb Agreement*

I. Some **nouns** which are *plural* in form (that is, in spelling), are *singular* in usage (that is, they take a singular verb). Frequently, these types of nouns are related to *money, periods of time, weights,* or *measurements.*

> **Examples:**   1. *Six dollars **seems*** too much to pay for such a small kit.
>
> 2. *Fourteen days **is*** the normal incubation period for some diseases.
>
> 3. A *thousand pounds* **is** not unusual for the weight of a young elephant.
>
> 4. *Three yards* of fabric **makes** a sizeable tablecloth.

II. The word **number** used as the subject of a sentence can be either *singular* or *plural.* If it is preceded by the article *the,* it is singular. If it is preceded by the article *a,* it is plural.

> **Examples:**   1. *The number* of bands entering the contest always **surprises** the judges.
>
> 2. *A number* of wild geese **fly** over our house every fall.

III. **Collective nouns** may be either *singular* or *plural.* If they are the antecedent of a plural pronoun, they must be considered plural and have a plural verb. If they are the antecedent of a singular pronoun, they must be considered singular and have a singular verb.

> **Examples:**   1. The *band **was playing*** its* spring concert.
>
> The *band **were wearing*** their* new uniforms.
>
> 2. The *jury **were expressing*** diverse opinions among *themselves.*
>
> The *jury **is rendering*** its* verdict.

IV. When sentences begin with the **adverbs** *here, there,* or *where,* the subject follows the verb, but the rules of subject-verb agreement remain in force. One must anticipate the number of the subject in choosing the verb. The same rule applies when *there* is replaced by other words (such as the *adverbial phrase* in Example 4 below), and the subject still follows the verb.

> **Examples:**   1. Here **come** our new *monitors.*
>
> 2. There **are** four *candidates* **running** for office.
>
> 3. Where **is** *Lake Geneva* **located**?
>
> 4. <u>Next to our school</u> *stands* an old oak tree. <u>Behind our house</u> *stand* several lilac bushes. (*The underlined portions are adverbial phrases.*)

Write sentences beginning with the following groups of words. Be sure the verbs agree with their subjects in number. Use the present tense for all your verbs. Use action verbs wherever possible.

1. Sixteen feet of grass _____

    _____

2. Here goes _____

    _____

3. Doesn't the team _____

    _____

4. Some of the music _____

    _____

5. Two thirds of the sheep _____

    _____

6. A number of _____

    _____

7. There appear _____

    _____

8. Don't the _____

    _____

9. The number _____

    _____

10. Fifty pounds of _____

    _____

11. Neither the band nor the choir _____

    _____

12. Either of the _____

    _____

13. Where do _____

    _____

14. The crowd _____

    _____

15. Each of the _____

    _____

16. Every one of the _____

    _____

17. Seven dollars _____

_____

18. Six weeks _____

_____

19. The clerk and typist (one person) _____

_____

20. Doesn't most of the _____

_____

21. All of the contents _____

_____

22. There stand _____

_____

23. Cereal and milk (a single unit) _____

_____

24. Weren't some of the _____

_____

25. Aren't all of the _____

_____

Lesson Sixteen

◆ *Subject-Verb Agreement in Adjective Clauses*

I. **Relative pronouns** (*who, whom, which, whose, that*) referring to plural antecedents require plural verbs; relative pronouns referring to singular antecedents require singular verbs. (Reminder: relative pronouns begin adjective clauses.)

   Examples: 1.   The clubs have their own *rules*, which **govern** all club operations.

   2.   Our town has an excellent *library*, which **attracts** many patrons.

II. The above principle becomes troublesome when the sentence includes the phrase *one of*.

   A.   In sentences using the phrase *one of those who, one of those that*, or *one of those which*, check carefully to determine which word in the sentence is the *true* antecedent of the relative pronoun. Putting the *of* phrase first will sometimes help.

   Examples: 1.   I am one of those *people who* **like** to sing.

   (Of those people who **like** to sing, I am one.)

   2.   Easter is one of the most important *dates that* **grace** the calendar.

   (Of the dates that **grace** the calendar, Easter is one of the most important.)

   B.   If the article *the* precedes *only one*, the relative pronoun and verb are singular.

Examples: 1. She was *the only one* of those attending *who* **understands** the issue.

2. Oranges are not *the only one* of the fruits *which* **has** vitamin C.

III. Subjects are sometimes followed by parenthetic expressions that are called **interrupters**. These expressions are related to the subject in meaning but do not affect its number.

Examples: 1. The *team*, together with the band, **arrives** as early as possible.

2. The *uniforms*, as well as the music, **are stored** in the music room.

Rewrite the following sentences, inserting the italicized words at the points indicated by the carets. Below the sentences, write the subject and verb of the rewritten sentence, as well as the number of the subject and verb. In rewritten sentences with **adjective clauses**, the student should write the subject and verb of the *dependent clause* in the blanks below the sentences, **not** the subject and verb of the independent clause.

Examples: Some ∧ arrives by mail. {*of our Christmas presents*}
Some of our Christmas presents arrive by mail.

subject **_Some_**   verb **_arrive_**   number **_plural_**

Neither ∧ lasts very long. {*of the practices*}
Neither of the practices lasts very long.

subject **_Neither_**   verb **_lasts_**   number **_singular_**

Cutting the grass ∧ takes two hours. {*and trimming the shrubbery*}
Cutting the grass and trimming the shrubbery take two hours.

subject **_Cutting, trimming_**   verb **_take_**   number **_plural_**

1. Is there a ∧ time specified in the contract? {*current and future*}

_____

_____

subject _____   verb _____   number _____

2. The purchase ∧ of American flags is popular now. {*and display*}

_____

_____

subject _____   verb _____   number _____

3. That beautiful sports arena ∧ makes a great attraction for national television. {*together with enthusiastic fans*}

_____

_____

subject _____   verb _____   number _____

4. Every major television network ∧ converges on the city. {*newspaper columnist, and radio announcer*}

_____

_____

   subject _____   *verb* _____   *number* _____

5. Either broadcaster ∧ is welcome at the stadium. {*or writer*}

_____

_____

   subject _____   *verb* _____   *number* _____

6. Don't ∧ the computers have the same program?{*each of*}

_____

_____

   subject _____   *verb* _____   *number* _____

7. Each reporter ∧ has his or her own style for describing the event. {*whether for radio, television, or a newspaper*}

_____

_____

   subject _____   *verb* _____   *number* _____

8. Twenty-five dollars for a ticket ∧ was a steep price to pay for many fans. {*and a reserved seat*}

_____

_____

   subject _____   *verb* _____   *number* _____

9. The eruption of a volcano ∧ frightens nearby residents. {*and its flow of lava*}

_____

_____

   subject _____   *verb* _____   *number* _____

10. Three inches of yardage ∧ often requires much skill for a football team. {*for a first down*}

_____

_____

   subject _____   *verb* _____   *number* _____

11. The number ∧ coming early always intrigues me. {*of fans, reporters, and photographers*}

_____

_____

  subject _____   *verb* _____   *number* _____

12. My friend ∧ arrives late. {*is not the only one of my classmates who*}

_____

_____

  subject _____   *verb* _____   *number* _____

13. The series ∧ lasts for a week. {*of games*}

_____

_____

  subject _____   *verb* _____   *number* _____

14. Most ∧ tastes fresh. {*of the peanuts*}

_____

_____

  subject _____   *verb* _____   *number* _____

15. One bluebird ∧ builds a nest in my backyard every summer. {*or maybe two*}

_____

_____

  subject _____   *verb* _____   *number* _____

16. A number ∧ land with precision timing. {*of planes and helicopters*}

_____

_____

  subject _____   *verb* _____   *number* _____

17. The number ∧ disturbs me. {*of errors in my math computations*}

_____

_____

  subject _____   *verb* _____   *number* _____

18. The decision ∧ disappoints us. {*of the committee and its ruling*}

_____

_____

subject _____   verb _____   number _____

19. Don't ∧ the animals need better care? {*each of*}

_____

_____

subject _____   verb _____   number _____

20. We bought one ∧ that needs some new paint. {*of the deck chairs*}

_____

_____

subject _____   verb _____   number _____

21. Neither ∧ yields a prolific crop. {*the fruit trees nor the grapevines*}

_____

_____

subject _____   verb _____   number _____

22. My brother ∧ does excellent work. {*is only one of the athletes who*}

_____

_____

subject _____   verb _____   number _____

23. The candidate for senator ∧ announces early. {*is the only one of the men who*}

_____

_____

subject _____   verb _____   number _____

24. That dachshund ∧ eats everything. {*is not the only one of the dogs which*}

_____

_____

subject _____   verb _____   number _____

25. Aren't ∧ the classrooms beautifully carpeted? {*each of*}

_____

_____

subject _____   verb _____   number _____

26. Don't ∧ the different books explain the concept clearly? {*every one of*}

_____

_____

subject _____   verb _____   number _____

27. There go ∧ the elephants. {*one of*}

_____

_____

subject _____   verb _____   number _____

28. A hundred pounds ∧ was hard to handle. {*of fertilizer and topsoil*}

_____

_____

subject _____   verb _____   number _____

29. Neither ∧ produces sufficient food. {*Russia nor Mexico*}

_____

_____

subject _____   verb _____   number _____

30. The president ∧ of the company provides insurance for his employees. {*and manager*}

_____

_____

subject _____   verb _____   number _____

Lesson Seventeen

◆ *Argumentative Paragraph*

In an **argumentative paragraph**, the writer *makes a statement* or *offers an opinion* and *gives reasons* to substantiate the statement or opinion. The writer may take either a positive or a negative position. The purpose of argumentation is to *persuade* or *convince*. The plan to follow in writing an argumentative paragraph is to list all the reasons for or against the position taken by the writer. These reasons may be given in order of descending or ascending importance or in any arbitrary order. Under each reason, facts or evidence is given to establish that particular point. The writer should guard against introducing irrelevant points, facts, or evidence that may tend to weaken his position, destroy the line of reasoning, or demonstrate illogical thinking. He should make all of his material lead to an inescapable conclusion. An alternative approach to argumentation is to present both sides of an argument and allow the reader to make his own decision.

Choose one of the following topic sentences and develop an argumentative paragraph.

1. The school year should (or should not) be extended to a full year.

2. Women should (or should not) have combat roles in war.

3. Freedom of speech (or Christian ethics) gives (or does not give) a speaker the right to criticize another publicly.

4. Televised debates between opposing candidates should (or should not) be required by law.

5. College athletes should (or should not) be paid a salary.

_____

_____

_____

_____

_____

_____

_____

_____

_____

_____

_____

_____

_____

_____

_____

_____

_____

_____

_____

_____

_____

Lesson Eighteen

◆ *Review of Noun Classification*

Review *Lessons 6, 7*, and *8*. Then, without referring to these lessons for help, identify the following classes of nouns and write examples illustrating each.

I. Common nouns _____

_____

People	Places	Things	Ideas, Qualities
1. _____	1. _____	1. _____	1. _____
2. _____	2. _____	2. _____	2. _____
3. _____	3. _____	3. _____	3. _____
4. _____	4. _____	4. _____	4. _____
5. _____	5. _____	5. _____	5. _____

II. Proper nouns _____

_____

People	Places	Things	Ideas, Qualities
1. _____	1. _____	1. _____	1. _____
2. _____	2. _____	2. _____	2. _____
3. _____	3. _____	3. _____	3. _____
4. _____	4. _____	4. _____	4. _____
5. _____	5. _____	5. _____	5. _____

III. Compound nouns _____

_____

People	Places	Things	Ideas, Qualities
1. _____	1. _____	1. _____	1. _____
2. _____	2. _____	2. _____	2. _____
3. _____	3. _____	3. _____	3. _____
4. _____	4. _____	4. _____	4. _____
5. _____	5. _____	5. _____	5. _____

Lesson Nineteen

◆ *Review of Noun Classification*

Review *Lessons 6, 7,* and *8.* Then, without referring to any previous lesson for help, identify the following classes of nouns and write examples illustrating each.

I. Collective nouns _____

_____

1. _____	6. _____	11. _____	16. _____
2. _____	7. _____	12. _____	17. _____
3. _____	8. _____	13. _____	18. _____
4. _____	9. _____	14. _____	19. _____
5. _____	10. _____	15. _____	20. _____

II. Concrete nouns _____

_____

1. _____	6. _____	11. _____	16. _____
2. _____	7. _____	12. _____	17. _____
3. _____	8. _____	13. _____	18. _____
4. _____	9. _____	14. _____	19. _____
5. _____	10. _____	15. _____	20. _____

III. Abstract nouns _____

_____

1. _____	6. _____	11. _____	16. _____
2. _____	7. _____	12. _____	17. _____
3. _____	8. _____	13. _____	18. _____
4. _____	9. _____	14. _____	19. _____
5. _____	10. _____	15. _____	20. _____

Lesson Twenty

◆ *Practice with Subject-Verb Agreement*

Review *Lessons 9, 10, 15,* and *16,* which discuss agreement of subjects and verbs in number. Then, without reference to those lessons, complete the following exercise. Underline the subjects and correct verbs. Below each sentence, explain the grammatical rule or subject-verb-agreement concept that applies to that sentence.

Example: From where (<u>does</u>, do) your household <u>water</u> come?

<u>When the sentence is a question, the subject usually follows the verb and must be identified before the verb is chosen.</u>

1. A number of authors (spends, spend) years writing about national parks.

   _____

   _____

2. Two thirds [note: no hyphen] of the nation's park system (lies, lie) within the boundaries of Alaska.

   _____

   _____

3. Eight million acres of land (is, are) within the boundaries of the national parks.

   _____

   _____

4. Some activists claim that industrial development near the parks (threatens, threaten) wildlife.

   _____

   _____

5. Yosemite National Park is one of the national parks that (shows, show) evidence of high traffic.

   _____

   _____

6. Some of the parks (was, were) established to preserve history.

   _____

   _____

7. Each lake, mountain trail, and wildlife refuge (tells, tell) its own story.

   _____

   _____

8. When (was, were) the original National Park Service Act signed?

   _____

   _____

9. Neither Congress, which passed the act, nor President Woodrow Wilson, who signed it, (was, were) able to envision how important national parks would be in the future.

    _____

    _____

10. There (was, were) only 36 parks in 1916.

    _____

    _____

Lesson Twenty-one

◆ *Practice with Subject-Verb Agreement*

Follow the directions in the previous lesson to complete the exercise below.

1. The number of parks (has, have) grown from 36 in 1916 to 357.

    _____

2. Not all of the areas administered by the Park Service (is, are) called parks.

    _____

3. Either camping or hiking (poses, pose) an opportunity to enjoy the parks.

    _____

4. Some of the Park Service responsibilities (includes, include) protecting natural treasures from hazards.

    _____

5. Every monument, seashore, river, and wildlife preserve (remains, remain) an enjoyable destination for a vacation visit.

    _____

6. Either (offers, offer) us much pleasure.

    _____

7. A careless crowd visiting a park often (does, do) damage to the landscapes.

    _____

8. A park ranger and manager (deserves, deserve) appreciation for his care of the natural resources in a park.

   _____

   _____

9. One half of the funds (is, are) spent on park clean-up.

   _____

   _____

10. Yellowstone is the oldest of the parks which (accommodates, accommodate) millions of sight-seers annually.

    _____

    _____

Lesson Twenty-two

◆ *Practice with Subject-Verb Agreement*

Follow the directions in the previous lesson to complete the exercise below.

1. Where (was, were) the first designated areas for parks?

   _____

   _____

2. Neither of them (was, were) east of the Mississippi.

   _____

   _____

3. Two weeks at Yellowstone (is, are) not enough time to see all of its wonders.

   _____

   _____

4. Out West (was, were) the beginnings of the parkland preservations.

   _____

   _____

5. Berries and cream (is, are) seldom sold as a dessert in concession stands in parks.

   _____

   _____

6. (Isn't, Aren't) an appreciation of our forefathers' wisdom appropriate?

   _____

   _____

7. Proposing which of nature's offerings are to be preserved and recommending finances for their protection (remains, remain) the charges of the National Park Service.

_____

_____

8. Neither the fishermen in the streams nor the climbers on the mountain slopes (wants, want) these resources abandoned by the Park Service.

_____

_____

9. Here in the United States (lies, lie) the world's largest recreational and sightseeing preserves.

_____

_____

Lesson Twenty-three

◆ *Spelling*

Learn to pronounce and spell the following words.

1. debris	6. devastating	11. maintenance
2. Philippines	7. eruption	12. numeral
3. volcanic	8. evacuated	13. underneath
4. impassable	9. accessibility	14. composition
5. Filipinos	10. geographical	15. designated

Lesson Twenty-four

◆ *Spelling and Vocabulary*

Learn to pronounce, spell, and identify the following words.

1. intensified	5. avalanche	9. dormant
2. ferocious	6. journalist	10. dachshund
3. volcano	7. plagiarism	11. eruption
4. pyroclastic	8. format	12. thesis

Lesson Twenty-five

◆ *Vocabulary*

Use words from *Lesson 24* to complete these sentences.

1. To lie _____ is to be inactive or asleep.

2. As the wind increased, the rain also _____.

3. Literary theft is called _____.

4. Mount Pinatubo is a _____ that lay dormant in the Philippines for 600 years before erupting in 1991.

5. Molten rock formed an _____ rushing down the mountainside.

6. The eruption was a blast with _____ intensity.

7. A flow of ash, dust, rock, and lava from a volcano is called a _____ flow.

8. A _____ covering a news event must be governed by a sense of fairness and objectivity.

9. News stories are often written according to a _____ known as the "inverted pyramid."

10. Military facilities 25 miles away were covered with a foot of ash billowing down from the _____ of Mount Pinatubo.

11. Writers must adequately develop their _____ statements when writing an essay or editorial.

12. Someone has said that a _____ is a canine which is one half of a dog high and two dogs long.

Lesson Twenty-six

◆ *Letter Writing*

Write a letter to the National Park Service, requesting information concerning one of the national parks or monuments in the United States. Your letter should contain the elements shown in the example below. Type the letter if you have access to a typewriter or computer. Use the following format.

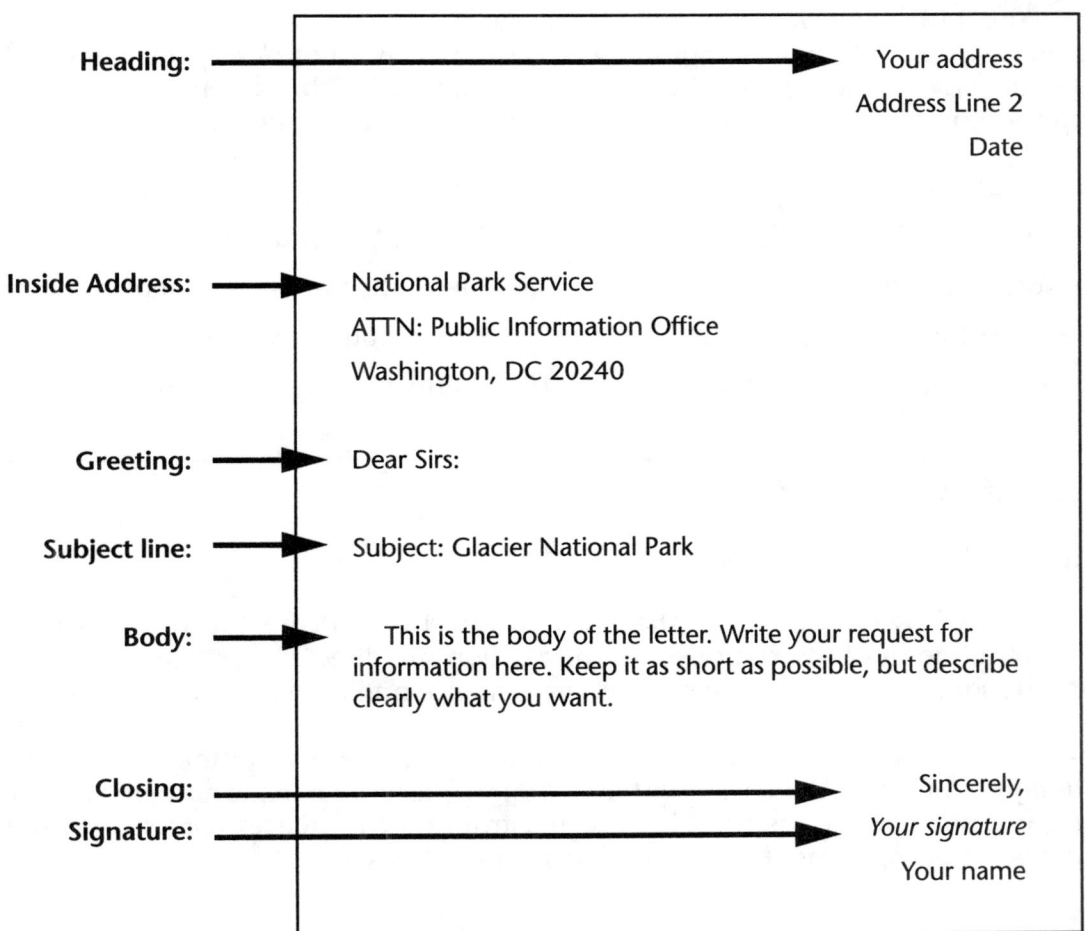

Follow this format in addressing your envelope.

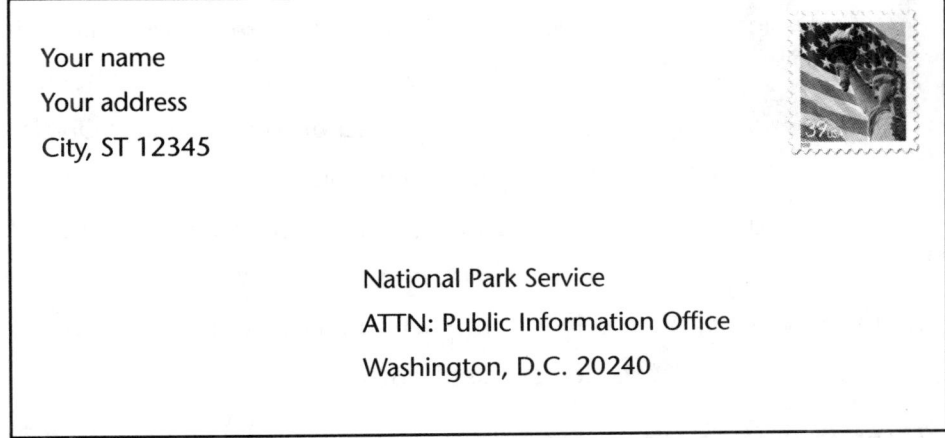

Lesson Twenty-seven

◆ *Descriptive Paragraph*

The names of some national parks and monuments are listed below. Choose one of them or any other national park, national monument, national historical park, national battlefield, or national recreation area that interests you. Learn all you can about it, and write a *descrip-*

tive paragraph about it. Do not copy sentences from the resource material you read, unless you enclose them in *quotation marks* and **cite the source**. Choose your *topic sentence* carefully so that anyone who reads your paragraph will know exactly what *clews* your paragraph will describe. With your teacher's permission, you may wish to delay this lesson until you receive a reply from the National Park Service to the letter you wrote in the previous lesson.

1. Yellowstone National Park
2. Grand Teton National Park
3. Yosemite National Park
4. Grand Canyon National Park
5. Great Smoky Mountains National Park
6. Crater Lake National Park
7. Acadia National Park
8. Mount Rushmore National Memorial
9. Effigy Mounds National Monument
10. Rainbow Bridge National Monument

Lesson Twenty-eight

◆ *Transitive and Intransitive Verbs*

Action verbs that have a receiver of their action (direct object) are called **transitive verbs**. Action verbs that do not have a receiver of their action (no direct object) are called **intransitive verbs**. The same verb can be *transitive* in one sentence and *intransitive* in another.

It is sometimes helpful in recognizing *transitive* and *intransitive verbs* to take note of the sentence's "design." Although the term "**sentence design**," as used here, is not one you will find in many grammar books, it is used here to illustrate how sentences consist of a series of "building blocks" or components arranged according to a design.

Examples:

Design A: *Subject + **Intransitive Action Verb***

The *wind **blew*** across the plain at a steady speed.

Design B: *Subject + **Transitive Action Verb** + Direct Object* (in active voice)

The *wind **blew*** debris across the plain at a steady speed.

Design C: *Subject + **Transitive Action Verb** + Indirect Object + Direct Object*

The heavy *rains **bring*** our *trees* good *moisture*.

Design D: *Subject + **Linking Verb** + Predicate Complement* (Adjective or Nominative)

*Rain **is** good* for crops. Our best *crop **was** corn*.

I. In *active voice*, the receiver of the action is always the **direct object**.

The *wind blew **debris*** across the plain.

II. In *passive voice*, the "passive" receiver of the action is the **subject** of the sentence. Only *transitive verbs* can be used in passive voice.

The **debris** was blown across the plain by the wind.

III. *Linking verbs* **do not** have *voice*, **nor** are they considered *transitive* or *intransitive*.

Study the sentences on the next page. Write A, B, C, or D in the blanks at the left to indicate which of the four sentence designs illustrated above applies to the following sentences. Double-underline (___) the subject of the sentence. Underline (___) the verb and check the correct box to identify it as either *action* or *linking*, and as either *transitive* or *intransitive*, if the verb is an action verb. If the verb is an action verb, also check a box to indicate whether the sentence is written in *passive* or *active voice*.

Examples:

<u>A</u>　1.　The <u>volcano had</u> not <u>erupted</u> for 600 years.

☑ action　　　　　☐ transitive　　　　☑ active

☐ linking　　　　　☑ intransitive　　　☐ passive

<u>D</u>　2.　The <u>volcano had been</u> dormant for many years.

☐ action　　　　　☐ transitive　　　　☐ active

☑ linking　　　　　☐ intransitive　　　☐ passive

___　1.　After many days of ferocious activity, the eruption finally stopped.

☐ action　　　　　☐ transitive　　　　☐ active

☐ linking　　　　　☐ intransitive　　　☐ passive

___　2.　All aircraft were grounded after the incident.

☐ action　　　　　☐ transitive　　　　☐ active

☐ linking　　　　　☐ intransitive　　　☐ passive

___　3.　More than 300 people lost their lives.

☐ action　　　　　☐ transitive　　　　☐ active

☐ linking　　　　　☐ intransitive　　　☐ passive

___　4.　The volcano was 4,795 feet deep.

☐ action　　　　　☐ transitive　　　　☐ active

☐ linking　　　　　☐ intransitive　　　☐ passive

___　5.　The volcano spewed ash, steam, dust, and rocks over the area.

☐ action　　　　　☐ transitive　　　　☐ active

☐ linking　　　　　☐ intransitive　　　☐ passive

___　6.　Damage was intensified by heavy rains.

☐ action　　　　　☐ transitive　　　　☐ active

☐ linking　　　　　☐ intransitive　　　☐ passive

___　7.　Impassable roads gave relief workers an additional obstacle.

☐ action　　　　　☐ transitive　　　　☐ active

☐ linking　　　　　☐ intransitive　　　☐ passive

___　8.　Scores of buildings collapsed during the eruption.

☐ action　　　　　☐ transitive　　　　☐ active

☐ linking　　　　　☐ intransitive　　　☐ passive

___　9.　Nearby towns and villages were covered with ash from the volcano.

☐ action　　　　　☐ transitive　　　　☐ active

☐ linking　　　　　☐ intransitive　　　☐ passive

___ 10. The army evacuated all dependents from the country.

    □ action   □ transitive   □ active

    □ linking   □ intransitive   □ passive

___ 11. Subic Bay Naval Base was the principal site for Navy operations in the South Pacific.

    □ action   □ transitive   □ active

    □ linking   □ intransitive   □ passive

___ 12. Clark Air Force Base is another military installation in The Philippines.

    □ action   □ transitive   □ active

    □ linking   □ intransitive   □ passive

___ 13. Filipinos waded knee-deep in volcanic ash after Mount Pinatubo erupted.

    □ action   □ transitive   □ active

    □ linking   □ intransitive   □ passive

Lesson Twenty-nine

◆ *Practice with Sentence Designs, Voice, and Transitive & Intransitive Verbs*

Follow the directions given in the previous lesson to complete the following exercise.

___ 1. The eruption covered cars within a 25-mile radius with a foot of volcanic ash.

    □ action   □ transitive   □ active

    □ linking   □ intransitive   □ passive

___ 2. Mount Unzen in Japan gave the surrounding landscape gas, ash, and rock.

    □ action   □ transitive   □ active

    □ linking   □ intransitive   □ passive

___ 3. Lava destroyed everything in its path.

    □ action   □ transitive   □ active

    □ linking   □ intransitive   □ passive

___ 4. Many homes burned to the ground.

    □ action   □ transitive   □ active

    □ linking   □ intransitive   □ passive

___ 5. The scientific name for this "liquid fire" is a pyroclastic flow.

    □ action   □ transitive   □ active

    □ linking   □ intransitive   □ passive

___ 6. It is heavy.

    □ action   □ transitive   □ active

    □ linking   □ intransitive   □ passive

___ 7. It runs rather than shoots.
- ☐ action
- ☐ linking
- ☐ transitive
- ☐ intransitive
- ☐ active
- ☐ passive

___ 8. Its speed is faster than that of a lava stream.
- ☐ action
- ☐ linking
- ☐ transitive
- ☐ intransitive
- ☐ active
- ☐ passive

___ 9. It is a glowing avalanche.
- ☐ action
- ☐ linking
- ☐ transitive
- ☐ intransitive
- ☐ active
- ☐ passive

___ 10. Sixteen journalists lost their lives from the eruption in Japan.
- ☐ action
- ☐ linking
- ☐ transitive
- ☐ intransitive
- ☐ active
- ☐ passive

___ 11. Japanese fled with their clothes in shreds.
- ☐ action
- ☐ linking
- ☐ transitive
- ☐ intransitive
- ☐ active
- ☐ passive

___ 12. The devastation brought the country a debris-strewn landscape.
- ☐ action
- ☐ linking
- ☐ transitive
- ☐ intransitive
- ☐ active
- ☐ passive

___ 13. Before 1991, Mount Unzen had been quiet for some time.
- ☐ action
- ☐ linking
- ☐ transitive
- ☐ intransitive
- ☐ active
- ☐ passive

Complete the following exercise by filling in the blanks with the correct answers.

1. Transitive verbs always have a _____ of their action.

2. In active voice, the receiver of a transitive verb's action is the _____.

3. In passive voice, the receiver of a transitive verb's action is the _____.

4. Name the components of a sentence constructed in:

Design A: _____

Design B: _____

Design C: _____

Design D: _____

5. In passive voice, the verb will always be ☐ transitive ☐ intransitive, but the receiver of the action will be the _____ of the sentence.

6. Intransitive verbs never have a _____ of their action.

7. Linking verbs are neither transitive nor intransitive. ☐ true ☐ false

8. Name two types of predicate complements. _____

Lesson Thirty

◆ *Research Paper*

A *research paper*, also known as a *term paper* or *research theme*, is a lengthy composition, usually at least 1,500 words, which summarizes the results of a student's reading or investigation on a selected subject. It is intended to be more than a simple report on a given book or other literary work. Its purpose is to lead the student into a thorough investigation of existing literature on the chosen subject and to interpretively present various source materials in light of the researcher's full investigation. The idea is to gather information from a variety of sources and compile the information into a unified message. The message includes the researcher's own words, along with quotations from the researcher's readings. Quotations are given proper credit in a format used by formal researchers. As one expert has said, "A good research paper is a study, carefully controlled, which sets out with a definite purpose and accomplishes that purpose."

There are **five major steps** to follow in writing a research paper. These are as follows:

1. **Choose, analyze, and limit your subject.**

    Select a subject in which you have some interest or in which you think you could develop an interest. Also keep reader interest in mind. A highly technical or obscure subject may interest you, but the average reader may not be so technically inclined. Your subject should not be overly broad or narrow. Subjects that are too general will result in a paper that lacks focus. Subjects that are too small often tempt the writer to "pad," repeat, or stray from the subject, with confusion or dullness the likely results. Be sure to choose a subject for which sufficient source material can be found in the resources available to you. You will be required to use *several kinds of sources*: reference books, magazines, books, newspapers, personal interviews, etc. Be sure the subject you choose is one about which various writers in these kinds of sources have previously written.

    Think about your subject in terms of what **controlling theme** or central purpose your research paper will have. Consider some specific proposition you will want to advance when your paper is written. You will be assembling your source material to support this central idea; so when you select your subject, be sure that it is one for which you will be able to find relevant documentation. Although you probably *cannot prepare a detailed outline* until you have done your research, it is helpful to consider in advance and write down a *general preliminary plan* for your paper.

    Consider in advance which of the **four basic forms of writing** you will employ: *description, exposition, narrative,* or *argument*. Most likely, you will employ more than one of these forms in the course of your paper. Be prepared to find source material needed to make these forms of writing effective.

2. **Thoroughly investigate your subject.**

    Begin to **find your sources** by visiting a library or identifying other resources available to you. In a library, you will find index books, card catalogs, or electronic databases that have listings of books and periodicals. Some of these are arranged by subject, by author, or by publication name. Make *bibliography cards*, using 3-inch by 5-inch index cards. Use one card for each source. Number the cards in the upper right-hand corner.

A bibliography card for a **book** should look something like this:

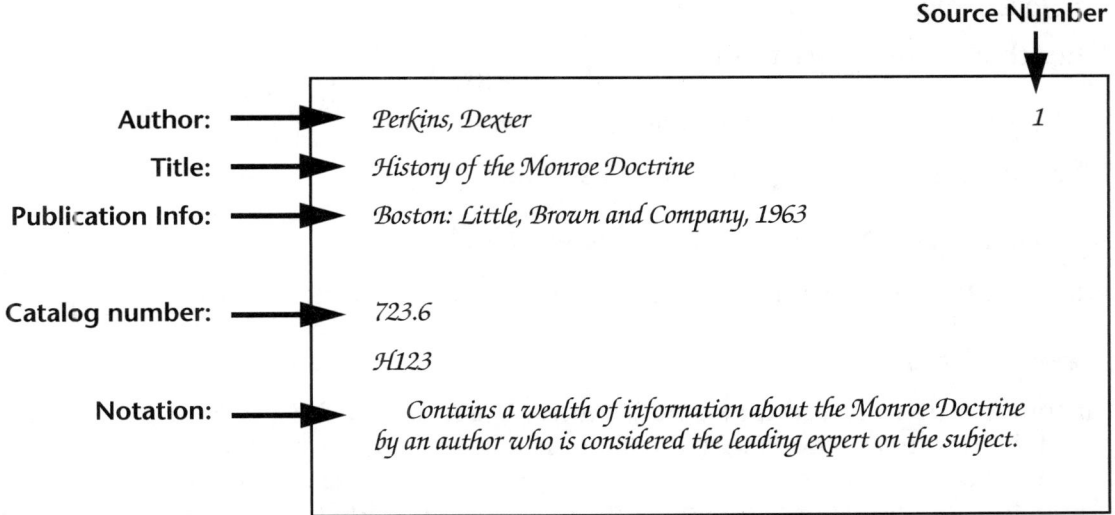

A bibliography for a **magazine article** should look something like this:

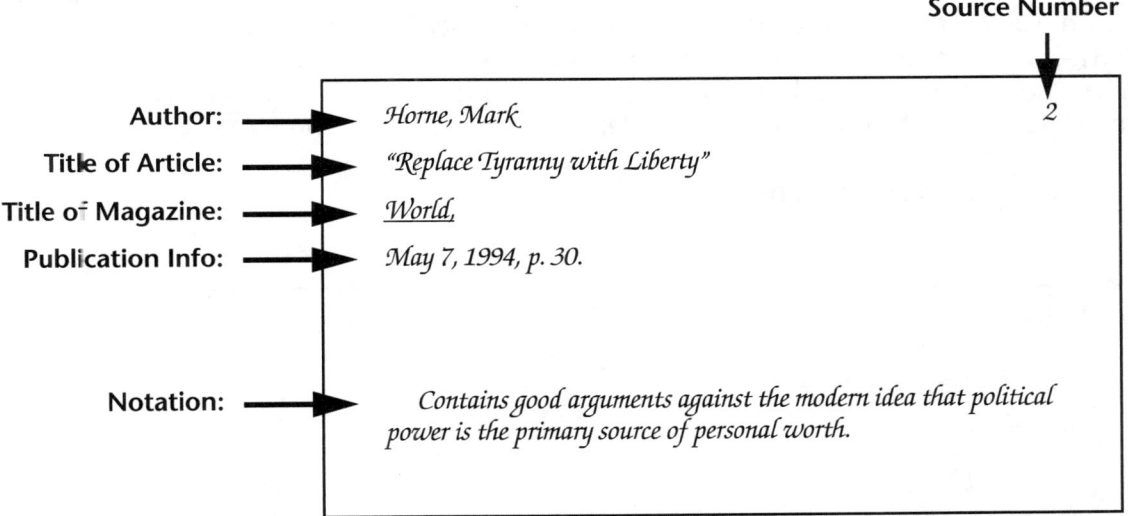

A bibliography card for an **encyclopedia article** should look something like this:

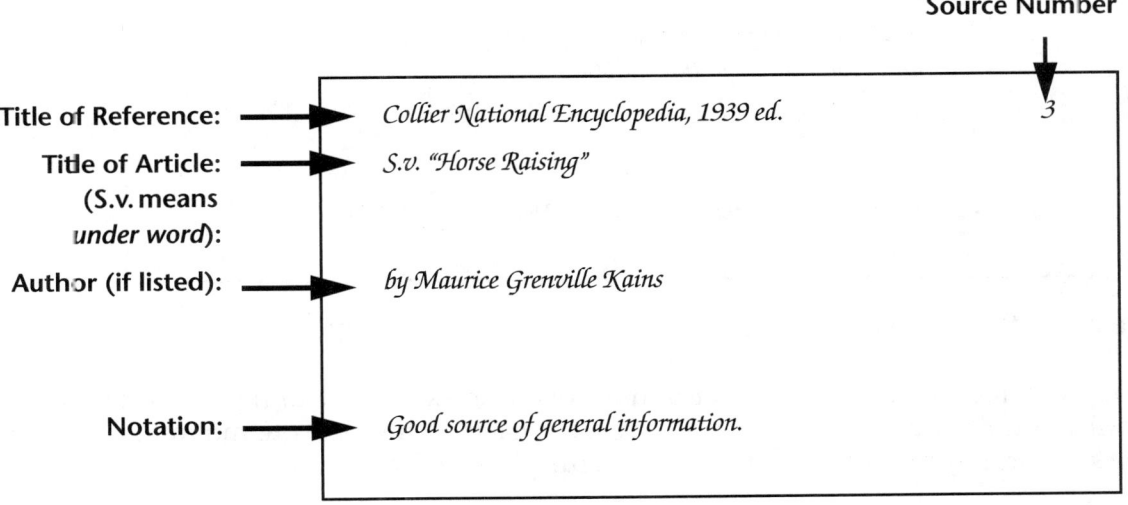

If a work has two authors, use this form:

> *Jones, Robert D., and John Smith.*

If a work has three authors, use this form:

> *Jones, Robert D., John Smith, and Mary J. Brown*

If a work has more than three authors, use this form:

> *Jones, Robert D., et al (et al means "and others")*

If a work lists only an editor's name on the title page, use this form:

> *Green, Michael, ed.*

Read your source materials and ***take careful notes***. Use index cards (3" x 5" or 4" x 6", according to your teacher's instructions). At the bottom of each note card, give full details of the source or use the *source number* from the upper right-hand corner of your bibliography card. Putting full details of your source on your note card will preclude the need for constant cross-referencing between **note cards** and **bibliography cards**. Be sure that any *quotations* you intend to use are placed on your note cards and written *accurately*. It is just as important that *paraphrases* be accurate. Get all the information you need from your first reading, if possible, so you do not need to search for the source material a second time. Place a *key word* in the upper right-hand corner of each note card to identify the subject of the note. Try to be as concise as possible. If a note is too lengthy to fit on one card, use more than one card and add a number or letter to the key word (for example, *Monroe 1, 2, 3* or *Monroe A, B, C*).

A note card should look something like this:

(Democracy)

Political power and personal worth

1. *Myths:*

    a. *Popular elections give political power to people*

    "Political power is always concentrated in the hands of a few. There can be no rulers unless someone is ruled." (p. 30)

    b. *Democracy justifies the laws that are made democratically.*

    "A law is vindicated not by the number of people supporting it, but by measuring up to the standards of justice." (p. 30)

2. *"The antidote to tyranny is liberty, not democracy." (p. 30)*

    _____

    Mark Horne, "Replace Tyranny with Liberty," World, May 7, 1994, p. 30.

---

3. Prepare an outline for your paper.

After you have read your source material and taken notes, *study your note cards* to recognize an organizational pattern among them. *Become familiar* with your note material and *arrange your notes* according to your preliminary general plan and any modifications to your plan that your research has uncovered. **Write an outline** after you have worked mentally with your notes long enough to have reached some conclusions about them and can see an overall structure. Your outline should have clear headings from which you can prepare *topic sentences* for your paragraphs. Keep in mind as you prepare your outline that the purpose of your research and your research paper is to find facts, arrange them, interpret them, and reach conclusions about them. A researcher is a *discover* and *reporter* of facts primarily. While his main purpose may not be to influence behavior among his readers, he must be able to sort out the truth of his subject matter and cause his reader to understand his purposes and conclusions. Of course, if argument is part of his approach, he may also wish to arrange his material so that the conclusion influences or persuades.

4. Write your paper.

Writing your paper takes several steps:

1. Write a *rough draft*. Include your footnotes in this first draft.

2. Reread your first draft and make handwritten *changes and revisions*.

3. Write *additional drafts* and *revisions* as necessary until your paper meets all your expectations and general requirements.

4. Write a *final draft*.

There is no reason for a research paper to be dull and lifeless. Write as expressively as possible. *Be clear, forceful, correct, and effective.* Revise the paper as many times as necessary. If you have sufficient time, set the paper aside occasionally for a few days; think about it; reread it; and rewrite it.

Footnotes should take the following forms (titles in *italics* below may be underlined if you are not using a typing system capable of producing italics). Note carefully the way the footnotes are punctuated.

For books (one author):

[1] Sidney Homer, *A History of Interest Rates*, 2nd ed. (New Brunswick, NJ: Rutgers University Press, 1977), pp. 3-4.

For books (multiple authors):

[1] Donella Meadows, et al, *The Limits to Growth*, 2nd ed. (New York: Universe Books, 1974), p. 125.

For periodical articles:

[1] Raymond S. Duff and A.G.M. Campbell, "Moral and Ethical Dilemmas in the Special Care Nursery," *New England Journal of Medicine*, vol. 289, no. 17, Oct. 25, 1973, pp. 890ff.

For quotations by one author taken from a book by another author:

[1] John Maynard Keynes, *Essays in Persuasion*, p. 371, quoted in Herman Kahn and Anthony J. Wiener, *The Year 2000: A Framework for Speculation on the Next Thirty-Three Years* (London: Macmillan, 1967), p. 215.

For newspaper articles:

[1] "The U.S. and Its Critics," *The New York Times*, April 15, 1956, Section 4, p. 8.

For a contribution from a collection:

[1] Katherine Mansfield, "Bliss," *A Study of the Short Story*, Henry S. Canby and Alfred Dashiell, eds. (New York: Henry Hold and Company, 1935), p. 303.

Footnotes may also be used to give the reader additional or *parenthetical information* written by the paper's author but which does not fit smoothly within the main text of the paper, which is too lengthy to be inserted within parentheses in the main text, or which is not directly related to the sentence in the main text.

> **Example:** [1]It might also be noted here that if our problems are religious in nature, they cannot be solved by scientific means.

Some footnotes may use standard abbreviations to preclude unnecessary repetition or to save space. Some common ones are:

Ibid. Short for *ibidem*, Latin for "in the same place." If a footnote cites the same source as the footnote *immediately* preceding it, you may use *ibid.* instead of the full name of the author, title, and publication information. If the page (or volume number) is different from the one cited in the preceding footnote, add the new location information.

> **Example:** [1]*Ibid.*, p. 23.

Op. cit. Short for *opere citato*, Latin for "in the work cited." If a reference is once given in full, future citations of the same work (those not qualifying for *ibid.*) may use *op. cit.* Again, if a different page or volume is quoted, add the new information.

> **Example:** [1]*Op. cit.*, vol. II, p. 78.

Loc. cit. Short for *loco citato*, Latin for "in the place cited." If a reference is made in a footnote to the *exact* passage mentioned in another footnote not immediately preceding the current one, use *loc. cit.* Never follow *loc. cit.* with a new page number.

> **Example:** [1]Smith, *loc. cit.*

cf. Short for "compare." This abbreviation is used to suggest that the reader, by cross reference, make comparisons between two pieces of source material. If you merely want to direct the reader to additional new material not used by you, use *See.*

> **Example:** *See also Psalm 130.*

5. Prepare a bibliography.

A **bibliography** is a list of books, magazines, articles, or other reference works placed at the end of your manuscript. The works listed in a *selected bibliography* are those you wrote on your bibliography cards and cited in your footnotes. A *full bibliography* may also include works that you researched for your paper but did not actually cite or from which you did not quote in the text of your paper. You may also cite works related to the subject of your paper but which you did not read or research. Arrange the works in your bibliography alphabetically by author's name or by title if no author is cited. You should make *separate* bibliography sub lists for various categories of literary works: Books, Magazines, Reference Books, Interviews, etc.

The entries for bibliographies are similar to those for footnotes, except that (1) the first or only author's name is *reversed* and (2) *periods* are used instead of *commas*. If you use two or more separate works by the same author, it is not necessary to list the author's name repeatedly. Instead, use a series of dashes or hyphens, or a straight line, in place of the author's name after it has been given once.

SELECTED BIBLIOGRAPHY

Books:

Beisner, E. Calvin. *Prosperity and Poverty.* Westchester, IL: Crossway Books, 1988.

_____. *Prospects for Growth.* Westchester, IL: Crossway Books, 1990.

Magazine Articles:

Boom, Monique. "Saudi Arabia: Severe Persecution." *Dorcas Journal.* March 1994.

Horne, Mark. "Replace Tyranny With Liberty." *World.* May 7, 1994.

Completion of your research paper will likely take several weeks or months. Therefore, you may proceed with the remaining lessons in this book while you are working on your research paper.

Lesson Thirty-one

◆ Spelling

Learn to pronounce and spell the following words.

1. archaeological	6. noticeable	11. dominating
2. introductory	7. formidable	12. ransack
3. normally	8. financially	13. missile
4. deteriorate	9. reservist	14. jeopardy
5. nonexistent	10. humiliation	15. personnel

Lesson Thirty-two

◆ Spelling and Vocabulary

Learn to pronounce, spell, and explain the following words.

1. crusade	8. infamous	15. ultimatum
2. traitor	9. anxiously	16. methodically
3. censor	10. reparation	17. colonize
4. eagerly	11. elliptical	18. inconceivable
5. Pentagon	12. ballistics	19. reconnaissance
6. emir	13. integrate	20. correlative
7. indelibly	14. collaborate	21. correspondent

Lesson Thirty-three

◆ *Vocabulary*

Use the vocabulary words from *Lesson 32* in the following sentences.

1. Because of the dangers, we _____ awaited some help.

2. Since we were sure we would win, our team _____ took the field.

3. The newspaper launched a _____ to arouse public attention to the problem of drunken driving.

4. The _____ is the headquarters for the U.S. Department of Defense.

5. Things that are naturally related are _____.

6. When an _____ is made by one party to a dispute, negotiations usually end and adverse action follows.

7. An _____ clause is one that has words understood but omitted.

8. A person who betrays another's trust is a _____.

9. A native ruler or chieftain in parts of Asia and Africa is an _____.

10. It is _____ how any ruler could order the deaths of his own people.

11. George Washington's legacy is _____ imprinted upon the pages of America's history and will never be erased.

12. If a book, article, or film has harmful or obscene material, a _____ may be called upon to remove the offending portions.

13. A person may be famous for his goodness or _____ for his evil.

14. The old church building was falling apart and was in need of _____.

15. It is considered treason to _____ with an enemy during a time of war.

16. _____ is the science of the motion of powder-propelled projectiles in flight.

17. The secretary carefully and _____ arranged the files according to a plan outlined in the company's office policy.

18. The judge ordered local officials to _____ the formerly segregated schools.

19. Ernie Pyle was a famous reporter and war _____ during World War II.

20. As part of its spying operation, the air force ordered _____ flights over the enemy's territory.

21. Several European countries attempted to _____ America during the first century after its earliest settlements.

Lesson Thirty-four

◆ *Compound Sentences*

An *independent clause* is a group of words:

1. including a subject and predicate,

2. forming a part of a sentence, and

3. making complete sense in themselves.

A *dependent clause* is a group of words:

1. including a subject and predicate,

2. forming a part of a sentence,

3. NOT making complete sense in themselves, but

4. depending upon an independent clause in the same sentence for its full meaning.

If a sentence contains only one complete thought and no dependent clauses, the sentence is called a *simple sentence*. A *compound sentence* contains at least two independent clauses but no dependent clauses. A *complex sentence* contains one independent clause and one or more dependent clauses. A *compound-complex* sentence contains two or more independent clauses and at least one dependent clause.

Compound sentences may be written and punctuated several different ways.

1. If the independent clauses are very short (three or four words), no punctuation is needed if the clauses are joined by a simple coordinating conjunction (*and, but, or, yet, nor, neither*).

    Example: The bombs fell and mass destruction followed.

2. The independent clauses in most compound sentences are joined by a *simple coordinating conjunction* and are separated by a *comma*.

    Example: The policeman warned the fleeing robber, but he defied the warning.

3. If one of the independent clauses contains *internal punctuation*, clauses joined by a simple coordinating conjunction are separated by a *semicolon*.

    Example: The Air Force, Navy, and Army were under the command of a single general; but each branch had its specific objectives.

4. Independent clauses that are **not** joined by a conjunction must be separated by a *semicolon*.

    Example: The pilots were ready to go; the orders were given to strike.

5. When independent clauses are joined by a *conjunctive adverb*, they must be separated by a semicolon. A comma must follow the conjunctive adverb if it is more than one syllable long. No comma is needed following a one-syllable conjunctive adverb.

    Examples: The control tower must coordinate flights; otherwise, collisions might occur.

    Originally, her name was Gluckstein; then it was changed to Gluck.

6. When independent clauses are joined by *correlative conjunctions*, they are separated by a comma.

   Example: Either you must leave immediately, or I will call the police.

   Learn and write these connecting words for compound sentences.

   Coordinating conjunctions:

   1. *and* _____   3. *or* _____   5. *neither* _____

   2. *but* _____   4. *nor* _____   6. *yet* _____

   Correlative conjunctions:

   1. *either...or* _____   3. *both...and* _____

   2. *neither...nor* _____   4. *not only...but also* _____

   Conjunctive adverbs:

   1. *also* _____   13. *besides* _____

   2. *likewise* _____   14. *furthermore* _____

   3. *moreover* _____   15. *indeed* _____

   4. *however* _____   16. *nevertheless* _____

   5. *still* _____   17. *nonetheless* _____

   6. *anyhow* _____   18. *otherwise* _____

   7. *therefore* _____   19. *henceforth* _____

   8. *so* _____   20. *consequently* _____

   9. *hence* _____   21. *as a result* _____

   10. *in fact* _____   22. *namely* _____

   11. *thus* _____   23. *for example* _____

   12. *that is* _____   24. *similarly* _____

Lesson Thirty-five

◆ *Practice with Correlative Conjunctions*

Conjunctions are words (or groups of words) that join words, phrases, or clauses. There are two classes of conjunctions: *coordinating* and *subordinating*. *Coordinating conjunctions* join elements that are of equal grammatical rank. *Subordinating conjunctions* join elements—specifically, clauses—of *unequal* grammatical rank; that is, they join dependent clauses (noun or adverb clauses) to independent clauses in complex sentences.

Connecting words considered *coordinating* include *simple conjunctions* (*and, but, or,* etc.); *conjunctive adverbs*; and *correlative conjunctions*. In this lesson, we will concentrate on correlative conjunctions.

Correlative conjunctions are connecting words used in pairs. They indicate the *relationship* between two grammatical elements or ideas expressed in a sentence. To be used properly, correlative conjunctions must connect elements that are parallel; that is, of the same grammatical form. The rule is: *ideas that are logically parallel should be **structurally parallel**.*

Examples:

Wrong: *Either* the *president* signs bills passed by Congress *or vetoes* them.

In the sentence above, the correlative conjunctions join a noun, "president," the subject of the sentence, with a verb, "vetoes."

Correct: The president *either* signs bills passed by Congress or *vetoes* them.

Correlative conjunctions should be used to correlate *only two ideas*. Since they are used in *pairs*, it is only logical that they be used to connect or correlate no more than two ideas or sentence elements.

Examples:

Wrong: *Both* my uncle, my aunt, *and* my cousins will be visiting us.

It appears that *either* the Giants, the Dodgers, *or* the Pirates will win the National League pennant.

English grammar usually recognizes only four pairings as true *correlative conjunctions*: *both...and, either...or, neither...nor,* and *not only...but also*. Sometimes other pairs are listed as *correlative conjunctions*, but careful study of their use usually indicates that their function is one of *subordinating,* not *coordinating*. For example, some people mistakenly consider *whether...or* to be a correlative conjunction, as in the sentence: *Whether* I read *or* don't depends upon what books are available. In reality, this sentence uses a *simple coordinating conjunction,* **or,** to connect two dependent (noun) clauses beginning with the *subordinating conjunction (signal word),* **whether,** one being implied: *Whether* I read *or* (whether I) don't (read) depends upon what books are available. Other pairs that sometimes appear to have a coordinating function, but which are **not** correlative conjunctions are the following: *just...so, though...yet, as...as, so...as, the more...the more, the more...the less, no sooner...than.*

Write eight sentences containing correlative conjunctions (two sentences for each pair).

1. _____

   _____

2. _____

   _____

3. _____

   _____

4. _____

   _____

5. _____

   _____

6. _____

   _____

7. _____

   _____

8. _____

   _____

Lesson Thirty-six

◆ *Conjunctive Adverbs*

Certain words classified as *adverbs* are usually used parenthetically in sentences. For example, the word in bold type in the following sentence is a parenthetical adverb modifying the verb: *He wishes, **however**, to express his regrets.* These same words may also be used to relate *two independent clauses or two sentences.* When used in this way, these adverbs are called **conjunctive adverbs**. As such, they are *coordinating* words; that is, they join elements that are of equal grammatical rank. To repeat, the only proper function of *conjunctive adverbs* is to join two independent clauses or two sentences. They are *misused* when they are made to join words, phrases, or dependent clauses.

Wrong:	My favorite sports are baseball and football, *also* volleyball.
	I mowed the lawn for an hour, *then* slept.
	I like green beans, *however* not peas.
Correct:	My favorite sports are baseball and football; *also,* I enjoy volleyball.
	I mowed the lawn for an hour; *then* I slept.
	I like green beans; *however,* I do not like peas.

Use a semicolon to separate coordinate independent clauses joined by a conjunctive adverb or conjunctive adverb phrase. Place a comma after the conjunctive adverb if it has two or more syllables. If the conjunctive adverb has only one syllable, no comma is needed following it. (*See examples above.*)

Study the list of conjunctive adverbs in *Lesson 34*. In the blanks that follow, write sentences using half of those conjunctive adverbs. Use each only once.

1. _____

   _____

2. _____

   _____

3. _____

   _____

4. _____

_____

5. _____

_____

6. _____

_____

7. _____

_____

8. _____

_____

9. _____

_____

10. _____

_____

11. _____

_____

Lesson Thirty-seven

◆ *Practice with Conjunctive Adverbs*

Refer again to the list of *conjunctive adverbs* in *Lesson 34*. Write sentences in the following blanks, using the eleven conjunctive adverbs you did not use in your sentences for the previous lesson.

1. _____

_____

2. _____

_____

3. _____

_____

4. _____

_____

5. _____

_____

6. _____
   _____

7. _____
   _____

8. _____
   _____

9. _____
   _____

10. _____
    _____

11. _____
    _____

Lesson Thirty-eight

◆ *Subordinating Conjunctions*

Subordinating conjunctions have only one use in a sentence: to connect a dependent clause (usually adverbial) to an independent clause.

Here is a list of *subordinating conjunctions*:

1. whereupon	12. till	23. whereas	34. until
2. although	13. as long as	24. whether	35. before
3. else	14. as soon as	25. only	36. after
4. except that	15. where	26. for	37. whither
5. so that	16. wherever	27. in order that	38. whence
6. since	17. if	28. because	39. though
7. as	18. as if	29. that	40. although
8. why	19. unless	30. inasmuch as	41. as though
9. than	20. provided	31. as...as, so...as	42. lest
10. when	21. providing	32. now that	43. notwithstanding the fact that
11. whenever	22. provided that	33. while	44. in so far as

NOTE: Adjective clauses, dependent clauses that modify nouns or pronouns, are joined to independent clauses by *relative pronouns*, which you probably have studied earlier in your English coursework. Adverbial clauses are dependent clauses introduced by a subordinating conjunction and functioning as adverbs. Some of the words listed above that serve as subordinating conjunctions in adverbial clauses may also be used to introduce noun clauses. When they do, they are usually called simply *signal words*, although some textbooks consider them subordinating conjunctions since they connect a *subordinate* (*dependent*) *clause* to an independent clause.

Examples:

Noun clauses: No one knows **why** *he did not come.*

His idea, **that** *everyone in the choir wear black and white*, was accepted by all.

Where *you attend college* may have a profound effect on your thinking.

Adverb clauses: **Whereas** *you have ignored my advice*, I shall ignore your request.

He admired her, **though** *he never told her of his feelings.*

Notwithstanding the fact that *you are young*, you have shown great maturity.

The use of the italicized words in the following sentences constitutes *faulty diction*. Rewrite the sentences, properly using *subordinating conjunctions* or *clause signals* in place of the misused words.

1. *Being as how* she was a girl, the boys would not allow her on their team.

   _____

   _____

2. Some people try to act *like* they are movie stars.

   _____

   _____

3. I do not believe *as how* I can entrust this job to you.

   _____

   _____

4. I read in the newspaper *where* the city council lost its chairman.

   _____

   _____

5. He never calls his mother *without* he thinks she will send him some money.

   _____

   _____

6. *Being that* I am an agreeable person, I will not take issue with your assessment.

   _____

   _____

7. My feet felt *like* they weighed a ton.

   _____

   _____

8. She cannot play the piano well *except* she practices every day.

_____

_____

Introductory adverbial clauses must be followed by a *comma*. Normally, adverbial clauses that come *after* an independent clause are not *preceded* by a comma unless the adverbial clause begins with the subordinating conjunction *for*, meaning *because*.

Write six sentences of your own with *adverbial clauses* in them.

1. _____

_____

2. _____

_____

3. _____

_____

4. _____

_____

5. _____

_____

6. _____

_____

Lesson Thirty-nine

◆ *Practice with Subordinating Conjunctions*

Rewrite the following sentences, putting an *adverbial clause* in each of them. Try to use different subordinating conjunctions in each sentence.

Example: A malfunction in the machine had not been apparent, and several injuries resulted.

Because a malfunction in the machine had not been apparent, several injuries resulted.

1. Incoming missiles were destroyed in the air, but falling debris damaged buildings and injured people.

_____

_____

2. An investigation of the crime was completed, and the families of the victims were informed of the results.

_____

_____

3. Thirty-five children became ill. School officials sought ways to prevent spread of the disease.

_____

_____

4. One single approach will not solve the problem. A combination of methods should be tried.

_____

_____

5. The company has created a department for finding solutions. It has become a "clearing-house" for developing new policy ideas.

_____

_____

6. We will not be free from disease, but our bodies will be renewed when we reach heaven.

_____

_____

7. Men and equipment began to return to their base. The war was over.

_____

_____

8. Evil tyrants rule, and the safety of righteous men is threatened.

_____

_____

Lesson Forty

◆ *Variations with Adverb Clauses*

The subordinating conjunction *as...as* offers some possibilities for variety in the use of adverbial clauses. When the first *as* is omitted but implied, some adverbial clauses can appear to begin with a predicate adjective or an *-ly* adverb.

Examples: (As) *Serious* as he was, the audience could not help noticing his comical bow tie.

(As) *Defiantly* as Goliath spoke, he could not withstand the power of God.

Some adverbial clauses may also *appear* to begin with *verbs*, usually *helping verbs*, in nontraditional constructions such as those below. Note that in these sentences, however, the subordinating conjunction *if* is implied:

Examples: *Had he believed* otherwise, he would have said so. (*If* he had believed otherwise....)

Should he *be elected*, he could become the best governor we have ever had. (*If* he should be elected....)

Could she *make* amends, she would gladly do it. (*If* she could make amends....)

Had he the possibility to live his life over, he would live it differently. (*If* he had the possibility....)

Rewrite the following sentences, using adverbial clauses constructed with one of the variants discussed above in each sentence.

1. The missile was successful in its initial use, but a malfunction in its guidance system was soon detected.

   _____

   _____

2. The Evanston Bulldogs were our chief rivals, but we performed well against them.

   _____

   _____

3. Scientific developments are phenomenal, but scientists are not infallible.

   _____

   _____

4. The commanders quickly conferred, and the battle plans began to take shape.

   _____

   _____

5. If good men should overlook tyranny, liberty will soon be lost.

   _____

   _____

6. If doctors were to value life more highly, fewer abortions would be performed.

   _____

   _____

7. We eagerly await peace, but obstacles remain in its path.

   _____

   _____

8. Mr. Cheney was capable. However, he was never promoted.

   _____

   _____

Lesson Forty-one

◆ *Elliptical Clauses*

When the subject of an adverbial clause refers to the same person, place, thing, or idea as the subject of the independent clause in the same sentence, the subject (and sometimes part of the predicate) of the adverbial clause may be omitted and implied. Such adverbial clauses are called ***elliptical clauses***.

Examples: Although he was weak, he struggled to complete the race.
Although weak, he struggled to complete the race.

While they were in prison, the prisoners of war recited Scripture verses.
While in prison, the prisoners of war recited Scripture verses.

When George was home for Christmas, he visited his old friends.
When home for Christmas, George visited his old friends.

NOTE: In the last example above, when the noun "George" in the adverbial clause was dropped, it was inserted into the main clause, replacing the pronoun "he." This was necessary for clarity of meaning because the sentence was standing alone in this example. In the context of a larger paragraph, such a change might not be necessary.

Elliptical clauses go awry when the omitted parts are not the same as their counterparts in the main clause.

Wrong: When singing a song, the piano must be in tune.
While casting your ballot, the voting-booth curtain should be closed.

Underline the subjects in both the adverbial clause and the main clause in the following sentences. Then rewrite the sentences, making *elliptical clauses* out of the adverbial clauses. If the subjects of the two clauses do not refer to the same thing, an elliptical clause cannot be used. In such cases, leave the blanks empty.

1. While the United Nations was voting to use military force, it was trying to enforce sanctions designed to prevent the use of force.

   _____

   _____

2. The police commandos were assigned specific positions while they were preparing to flush out the sniper.

   _____

   _____

3. The machine works well if it is kept free of dirt.

   _____

   _____

4. A motor will deteriorate quickly when it is not maintained properly.

   _____

   _____

5. His ability as a mechanic was obvious even though he lacked experience.

   _____

   _____

6. The pilots flew training missions while they were waiting for combat assignments.

   _____

   _____

7. Although Mr. Kelly was of retirement age, he continued to work for five more years.

_____

_____

8. Mrs. Grayson worked on her knitting project while she was waiting for the bus.

_____

_____

9. Though Greg never accepted his parents' advice as being wise, he complied with their rules.

_____

_____

10. Whenever my friends from my former home town visit my house, we recall the good times we once had together.

_____

_____

Lesson Forty-two

◆ *Practice with Clauses*

The following exercise is designed to demonstrate another method of adding variety to your writing through sentence structure and the creative use of *clauses*. Each of the following sentences contains both an *adverbial clause* and a *noun clause*. Rewrite each of the sentences placing the adverbial clause within the noun clause.

Example: (*In the following example, the noun clause is underlined, and the adverbial clause is printed in italics.*)

Michelle believed <u>that James would never admit his error</u> *even though he had stopped his sinful behavior.*

Michelle believed <u>that</u> *even though James had stopped his sinful behavior* <u>he would never admit his error.</u>

(*A common error with this type of construction is to repeat the **that** which introduces the noun clause. Be sure to avoid this error.*)

Wrong: Michelle believed **that** *even though James had stopped his sinful behavior* **that** he would never admit his error.

1. Some politicians believe that economic sanctions will make dictators behave better if the world can wait long enough.

_____

_____

2. The team marvelled that the game had gone so well even though there had been little time for practice.

_____

_____

3. Some people wish that nations would be more willing to negotiate when international problems arise.

_____

_____

4. Others believe that this will never happen so long as power is glorified.

_____

_____

5. Some Americans believe that democracy would help wherever the people of a land are willing to give it a chance.

_____

_____

6. Some men do not care that other people suffer whenever they pursue their own selfish goals.

_____

_____

7. Mature men confess that material possessions have profited them nothing when they took them unlawfully.

_____

_____

8. Some rulers think that the world will bow its knee to them if they can amass a large arsenal.

_____

_____

Lesson Forty-three

◆ Spelling

Learn to pronounce and spell the following words.

1. abbreviation	6. significance	11. systematically
2. indefinite	7. acceptably	12. factual
3. numerator	8. kindergarten	13. livable
4. denominator	9. interview	14. inconceivable
5. approximately	10. interior	15. uniformity

Lesson Forty-four

◆ *Spelling and Vocabulary*

Learn to pronounce, spell, and explain the following words.

1. tolerance
2. consecutive
3. collisions
4. illustrate
5. Anno Domini
6. execution
7. Fahrenheit
8. Celsius
9. respectively
10. acronyms
11. manuscript
12. pastoral
13. botany
14. continuity
15. coalition
16. contumacious
17. collaborate

Lesson Forty-five

◆ *Vocabulary*

Fill in the blanks in the following sentences with the words from *Lesson 44* that will make the sentences accurate and complete.

1. _____ is the scale on which the interval between the freezing point and the boiling point of water is 100°.

2. _____ is the scale on which the freezing point of water is 32° above zero and the boiling point is 212°.

3. The life of a shepherd or herdsman is _____.

4. _____ is the capacity to bear something unpleasant, painful, or difficult.

5. In their constant defiance of authority, the youthful gang members demonstrated a _____ spirit.

6. Good planning must be followed by proper _____ if desired goals are to be achieved.

7. Twelve pro-life organizations formed a _____ to promote legislation restricting abortion.

8. The winning ticket numbers were read aloud in _____ order from one to ten.

9. Flying jet fighters in formation requires great skill to avoid mid-air _____.

10. Our pastor would often _____ his sermons with anecdotes about his boyhood experiences on the farm.

11. _____, meaning "the year of the Lord," refers to the time within the Christian era that dates its beginning with the birth of Christ.

12. When Jan, Ashley, and Cody were age 12, 10, and 5, _____, their family moved to Cleveland.

13. Although three committees developed different aspects of the plan, there was a high degree of _____ among them which made execution of the plan efficient.

14. His _____ class taught him much about common vegetables.

15. Some companies, agencies, and groups are better known by their _____ than by their full names.

16. The novelist's _____ had not yet been submitted to his publisher.

17. It is treason to _____ with the enemy in a time of war.

Lesson Forty-six

◆ *Adjective Clauses*

Adjective clauses are dependent clauses that modify nouns or pronouns. Adjective clauses are introduced by words called relatives. There are two types of relatives—relative pronouns and relative adverbs.

Relative pronouns:

The most common **relative pronouns** are *who, whom, whose, which,* and *that.*

Less common relative pronouns are *whoever, whomever, whichever,* and *whatever.*

Relative pronouns that are now rarely used are *whosoever, whomsoever, whichsoever,* and *whatsoever.*

In addition to their function in the sentence—to introduce adjective clauses and thereby connect them to the main clause, relative pronouns have functions *within* the adjective clauses themselves:

> *Whom, whomever,* and *whomsoever* are used in adjective clauses in the same way as personal pronouns in the objective case are used; namely, as *direct objects, indirect objects,* or *objects of prepositions.*

> *Who, whoever,* and *whosoever* are used in adjective clauses in the same way as personal pronouns in the nominative case are used; namely, as *subjects* or *predicate nominatives.*

> *Whose* has the function of a possessive adjective within adjective clauses.

> *Which, that, whichever, whatever, whichsoever,* and *whatsoever* may be used in various cases. The possessive form of *which, etc.* is *of which, etc.*

Who, whom, whoever, and *whosoever* refer only to people.

Which refers only to things (inanimate objects) and animals.

That and *whose* are used in reference to animals, things, or people.

Relative pronouns have the *same form* in both *singular* and *plural*. Their number depends upon the number of their antecedents.

Relative adverbs:

The three most common *relative adverbs* are *when, where,* and *why.*

In addition to their function in the sentence—to introduce a dependent adjective clause and connect it to the main clause, relative adverbs have a function *within* the adjective clause—to modify the clause's verb.

Examples:

The ruler *who was forced into exile* returned in seven months.

> The adjective clause modifies the subject, *ruler.* **Who** is a relative pronoun in the nominative case. It introduces the clause and connects it to the main clause. It also serves within the clause as the clause's subject.

The suspect *whom the police accused* was a notorious gangster.

> The adjective clause modifies the subject, *suspect.* **Whom** is a relative pronoun in the objective case. It introduces the dependent adjective clause and connects it to the main clause. It also serves *within* the adjective clause as the direct object of the clause's verb, *accused.*

The refugees, *whose main needs were food, water, and medicine,* stood in line.

> The adjective clause modifies the subject, *refugees.* **Whose** is a relative pronoun in the possessive case. It introduces the dependent adjective clause and connects it to the main clause. It also serves *within* the adjective clause as an adjective modifying the subject of the clause, *needs.*

The gallery *where the artist displayed his work* is in New York.

> The adjective clause modifies the subject, *gallery.* **Where** is a relative adverb. It introduces the dependent adjective clause and connects it to the main clause. It also serves *within* the adjective clause as an adverb modifying the clause's verb, *displayed.*

Write sentences containing adjective clauses. Underline the words they modify. The clauses must begin with the relatives listed below. Remember that the clauses must modify nouns or pronouns in order to qualify as adjective clauses.

1. *who*   _____

   _____

2. *whom* _____

   _____

3. *where* _____

   _____

4. *that* _____

   _____

5. *whose* _____

_____

6. *which* _____

_____

7. *when* _____

_____

Lesson Forty-seven

◆ *Variety in Adjective Clauses*

The first word written or spoken in an adjective clause is not always a relative pronoun, due to alternative word orders in some cases. Here are four variations:

1. Sometimes the relative pronoun is *omitted* but *understood* or *implied*.

    Example: The man ~~whom~~ *I planned to meet* was late.

2. Sometimes indefinite pronouns such as *many, a few, one,* and *several* may precede *of which* or *of whom* at the beginning of an adjective clause.

    Examples: The men, ***two of whom*** *were German,* spoke good English.

    Ten zoo animals, ***most of which*** *were from Africa,* died today.

3. Sometimes the clause may begin with a noun or gerund (noun-like verbal), followed by a prepositional phrase having a relative pronoun as the object, such as *of which, of whom, for whom, through whom, by which,* etc.

    Examples: The solution, *the **formula for which** was unknown,* was stolen.

    The museum, *the **looting of which** was an international tragedy,* was closed for two weeks.

4. Sometimes the clause may begin with only a prepositional phrase with a relative pronoun as the object of the preposition.

    Examples: The people ***for whom*** *Christ died* are called "His beloved."

    The company ***through which*** *we shipped the container* is no longer in business.

Write two sentences illustrating each of the above variations in adjective clauses.

1. _____

_____

2. _____

_____

3. _____

_____

4. _____

_____

Lesson Forty-eight

◆ *Abbreviations*

Learn the following rules and guidelines for *abbreviations*.

1. **Time Zones**

    A. Eastern Standard Time, Eastern Daylight Time — EST, EDT

    B. Central Standard Time, Central Daylight Time —CST, CDT

    C. Mountain Standard Time, Mountain Daylight Time — MST, MDT

    D. Pacific Standard Time, Pacific Daylight Time — PST, PDT

    E. Greenwich Meridian (Mean) Time— GMT

2. **Time of Day**

    A. Ante Meridian—a.m. (midnight to noon)

    B. Post Meridian—p.m. (noon to midnight)

3. **Days and Months**

    Normally, **avoid** abbreviating in formal writing. In tabular material or other situations requiring abbreviation, use the following:

    Days of the Week: *Sun., Mon., Tues., Wed., Thurs., Fri., Sat.*

    Months: *Jan., Feb., March, April, May, June, July, Aug., Sept., Oct., Nov., Dec.*

4. **Business Terms**

    A. IOU (common term designating a debt—"I owe you"; use capital letters, no periods.)

    B. COD or c.o.d. (cash on delivery—payment due upon delivery of an item)

    C. FOB or f.o.b. (free on board—without charge for delivery at a specified point)

5. **Historical Dates**

    A. *anno Domini* ("in the year of our Lord")—A.D.

    Place A.D. *before* the number of the year: A.D. 70.

    B. "before Christ"—B.C.

    NOTE: Atheist secularists use the designation B.C.E., which stands for "before the Common Era."

    Place B.C. *after* the number of the year: 200 B.C.

6. **Weights, Measures, Capacities, Time Periods**

    Normally, avoid abbreviating in formal writing. In tabular material or other situations requiring abbreviation, use the following:

inch(es) = in.	hour(s) = hr., hrs.	bushel(s) = bu., bbl.
foot (feet) = ft.	month(s) = mo., mos.	milliliter = ml.
yard(s) = yd., yds.	year(s) = yr., yrs.	centiliter = cl.
acre = acre (or a.)	square = sq. (in., ft., yd., mi., etc.)	liter = l.
mile(s) = mi.	cubic = cu. (in., ft., yd., etc.)	teaspoon = teas., t
miles per hour = m.p.h.	grain = gr.	tablespoon(s) = tbl., tbls., T
millimeter = mm., mms.	dram = dr.	cup(s) = c.
centimeter = cm.	ounce(s) = oz.	fluid ounce = fl. oz.
meter = m.	pint(s) = pt., pts.	hundredweight = cwt.
kilometer = k.	pound(s) = lb., lbs.	ton = ton (or tn.)
kilometers per hour = k.p.h.	quart(s) = qt., qts.	gram = g.
second(s) = sec., secs.	gallon(s) = gal., gals.	kilogram = k.
minute(s) = min., mins.	peck(s) = pk., pks.	

7. *Temperature Scales*

Fahrenheit = F.   Celsius, Centigrade = C.

8. *Geographical Designations and Addresses*

Normally, **avoid** abbreviating in formal writing. In addresses or other situations requiring abbreviation, use the following (**capitalized** in names):

street = st.	river = r.
avenue = ave.	mountain(s), mount = mtn(s)., mt.
boulevard = blvd.	apartment, number = apt., no.
road = rd.	saint (in place name) = st.
court = ct.	fort (in place name) = ft.
lane = ln.	point (in place name) = pt.
drive = dr.	compass points = n., s., e., w., s.w., s.e.,
place = pl.	n.e, n.w., s.s.e, e.n.e., etc.

9. *Personal, Professional, Occupational, and Military Titles*

Normally, **avoid** abbreviating in formal writing. In situations requiring abbreviation, use the following, often capitalized:

mister(s) = Mr., Messrs. (always abbreviated)
mistress, mesdames (pl) = Mrs. or Ms., Mmes. (always abbreviated)
doctor(s) = Dr., Drs. (always abbreviated as a title before a name)
reverend, right reverend = Rev., Rt. Rev. (usually abbreviated as a title)
professor(s) = prof., profs.
president = pres.
vice president = v.p.
secretary = secy.
treasurer = treas.
assistant = asst.
representative, delegate = rep., del.
senator = sen.

(Continued at the top of the next page.)

assemblyman, assemblywoman = (do not abbreviate)
governor = gov.
lieutenant governor = lt. gov.
attorney(s) general = atty. gen., attys. gen.
director, executive director = dir., exec. dir.
chief executive officer = CEO

Military titles:

private = pvt.	colonel = col.
private first class = pfc.	brigadier general = brig. gen.
corporal = cpl.	major general = maj. gen.
specialist = spec.	lieutenant general = lt. gen.
sergeant = sgt.	general = gen.
lieutenant = lt.	commodore = (do not abbreviate)
captain = capt.	rear admiral = rear adm.
commander = cmdr.	vice admiral = vice adm.
major = maj.	admiral = adm.
lieutenant colonel = lt. col.	ensign = (do not abbreviate)
lieutenant junior grade = lt. j.g.	technical sergeant = tech. sgt.
lieutenant commander = lt. cmdr.	

10. Academic Degrees and Titles of Seniority *(In this manual, they have been alphabetized.)*

NOTE: *Abbreviate degrees, with or without periods, only following people's names. Spell out elsewhere in a sentence.*

bachelor of arts = B.A. (BA)	master of arts = M.A. (MA)
bachelor of science = B.S. (BS)	master of business administration = M.B.A. (MBA)
certified public accountant = C.P.A. (CPA)	master of science = M.S. (MS)
doctor of chiropractic = D.C. (DC)	master of social work = M.S.W. (MSW)
doctor of dental science = D.D.S. (DDS)	master of theology = Th.M. (ThM)
doctor of law(s) = LL.D. (LLD)	medical doctor = M.D. (MD)
doctor of optometry = O.D. (OD)	physician's assistant = P.A. (PA)
doctor of osteopathy = D.O. (DO)	registered nurse = R.N. (RN)
doctor of philosophy = Ph.D. (PhD)	
doctor of theology = Th.D. (ThD)	

doctor of theology = Th.D. (ThD)
emergency medical technician = E.M.T. (EMT)
licensed practical nurse = L.P.N. (LPN)
licensed vocational nurse = L.V.N. (LVN)

Titles of Seniority
junior = Jr.
senior = Sr.
the third, the fourth, etc. = III, IV, etc.

11. Names and Initials

Initials, followed by periods, for personal names are regularly used, as in *U. S.* Grant for *Ulysses Simpson* Grant.

Names are normally not abbreviated, except in footnotes, bibliographies, or other special uses. Some examples of names commonly abbreviated in such uses are:

Charles = Chas.	James = Jas.	William = Wm.
Benjamin = Benj.	Joseph = Jos.	Jonathan = Jon.

12. Names of U.S. States and Territories

Use the two-letter postal service abbreviations on the left in the table below when abbreviating *state*, *district*, or *territory* names in mailing addresses and in source citations. In any other writing that calls for abbreviations of state names, use the forms on the right.

AL	Alabama	Ala.	KY	Kentucky	Ky.	OH	Ohio	Ohio
AK	Alaska	Alaska	LA	Louisiana	La.	OK	Oklahoma	Okla.
AZ	Arizona	Ariz.	ME	Maine	Maine	OR	Oregon	Ore.
AR	Arkansas	Ark.	MD	Maryland	Md.	PA	Pennsylvania	Pa.
CA	California	Calif.	MA	Massachusetts	Mass.	PR	Puerto Rico	P.R.
CO	Colorado	Colo.	MI	Michigan	Mich.	RI	Rhode Island	R.I.
CT	Connecticut	Conn.	MN	Minnesota	Minn.	SC	South Carolina	S.C.
DE	Delaware	Del.	MS	Mississippi	Miss.	SD	South Dakota	S.D.
DC	District of Columbia	D.C.	MO	Missouri	Mo.	TN	Tennessee	Tenn.
FL	Florida	Fla.	MT	Montana	Mont.	TX	Texas	Tex.
GA	Georgia	Ga.	NE	Nebraska	Neb.	UT	Utah	Utah
GU	Guam	Guam	NV	Nevada	Nev.	VT	Vermont	Vt.
HI	Hawaii	Hawaii	NH	New Hampshire	N.H.	VI	Virgin Islands	V.I.
ID	Idaho	Idaho	NJ	New Jersey	N.J.	VA	Virginia	Va.
IL	Illinois	Ill.	NM	New Mexico	N.M.	WA	Washington	Wash.
IN	Indiana	Ind.	NY	New York	N.Y.	WV	West Virginia	W.Va.
IA	Iowa	Iowa	NC	North Carolina	N.C.	WI	Wisconsin	Wis.
KS	Kansas	Kan.	ND	North Dakota	N.D.	WY	Wyoming	Wyo.

13. United States, Agency Names

Abbreviate the name of the United States of America in addresses as: *U.S.A.* The abbreviation U.S. may be used as an adjective, as in *U.S. Department of State, U.S. foreign relations,* or *U.S. domestic policy.* Do **not** use the abbreviation *U.S.* as a **noun**, as in: *They traveled throughout the U.S. on their vacation.* Similarly, do not use *U.K.* as a noun in place of *United Kingdom.* Do **not** abbreviate *department* (*dept.*) or *division* (*div.*) in agency names.

14. Books of the Bible

Normally, do not abbreviate the names of the books of the Bible in sentences used in formal writing. However, in giving text citations, in footnotes, or in other situations requiring abbreviations, use the following forms:

Old Testament

Gen.	I Kings or 1 Kings	Eccles.	Amos
Exod.	II Kings or 2 Kings	Song of Sol.	Obad.
Lev.	I Chron. or 1 Chron.	or S. of S.	Jon.
Num.	II Chron. or 2 Chron.	Isa.	Mic.
Deut.	Ezra	Jer.	Nah.
Josh.	Neh.	Lam.	Hab.
Judg.	Esther	Ezek.	Zeph.
Ruth	Job	Dan.	Hag.
I Sam. or 1 Sam.	Ps.	Hos.	Zech.
II Sam. or 2 Sam.	Prov.	Joel	Mal.

New Testament

Matt.	II Cor. or 2 Cor.	I Tim. or 1 Tim.	II Pet. or 2 Pet.
Mark	Gal.	II Tim. or 2 Tim.	I John or 1 John
Luke	Eph.	Titus	II John or 2 John
John	Phil.	Philem.	III John or 3 John
Acts	Col.	Heb.	Jude
Rom.	I Thess. or 1 Thess.	James	Rev.
I Cor. or 1 Cor.	II Thess. or 2 Thess.	I Pet. or 1 Pet.	

15. **Use a period after every abbreviation**

There are a few exceptions to this rule. No periods are needed in the following cases:

   a. In contractions (*don't, isn't, aren't,* etc.)

   b. In abbreviated ordinal numbers (*1st, 2nd, 3rd, 4th,* etc.)

   c. After informally shortened words such as *math, phone, ad, exam, lab, TV,* etc.

   d. Call letters of broadcast stations: *KNBC, WBBM, WLS, KSL,* etc.

   e. Two-letter postal abbreviations in the United States and Canada (see No. 12 above): *CA, MI, BC, ON,* etc.

   f. Acronyms and abbreviations of certain agency names (see next lesson).

Lesson Forty-nine

◆ Acronyms

Acronyms are pronounceable "words" formed from the initial letters of key words in the names of organizations, agencies, government departments or divisions, unions, clubs, lobbying groups, movements, activities, technology, common ideas, etc. In some cases, the *acronym* is a stylized word or phrase only loosely following the full name of the group or idea.

Examples:

   NATO—**N**orth **A**tlantic **T**reaty **O**rganization

   UNESCO—**U**nited **N**ations **E**ducation, **S**cientific, and **C**ultural **O**rganization

   Yuppie—**Y**oung **U**rban **P**rofessional or **Y**oung **U**pwardly-mobile **P**rofessional

   SCSI—(pronounced "scuzzy") **S**mall **C**omputer **S**ystem **I**nterface

   Laser—**l**ight **a**mplification by **s**timulated **e**mission of **r**adiation

   AWOL—**A**bsent **W**ithout **L**eave

Although technically not acronyms—since they do not form "words"—other groups of initials are commonly recognized and often used without reference to the full names of the entities or ideas they represent. In the modern vernacular, these are also sometimes referred to as "acronyms."

Examples:

   ICU—**I**ntensive **C**are **U**nit

   AMA—**A**merican **M**edical **A**ssociation

   DJ—**D**isk **J**ockey

FBI—*F*ederal *B*ureau of *I*nvestigation

FAQ—*F*requently *A*sked *Q*uestions

In most cases, these acronyms and abbreviations are written entirely with *capital letters* and *without periods*. A few exceptions to the "all-caps" rule include such acronyms as *Fannie Mae*, abbreviation for *Federal National Mortgage Association*; *Jaycees*, name of an organization formerly called the *Junior Chamber of Commerce*; *emcee*, short for master of ceremonies; or *Caltrans*, abbreviation for the *California Department of Transportation*.

A few universally recognized acronyms may be used generally in most forms of writing. Some others may be acceptable in certain contexts. The use of acronyms is common in journalism. The world's largest news organization, The Associated Press, cautions its writers, however, to "avoid alphabet soup. Do not use abbreviations or acronyms which the reader would not quickly recognize." This is good advice for all writers. If you must use acronyms for the sake of brevity, spell out unfamiliar ones in your first reference and use the abbreviation in subsequent references.

In addition to the examples cited above, learn the following "acronyms" and their meanings.

AAA - American Automobile Association
AAD - Association of American Dentists
AARP - American Association of Retired Persons
AAU - Amateur Athletic Union
ABA - American Bar Association (lawyers' group)
ABC - American Broadcasting Company
ACE - Accelerated Christian Education
ACLU - American Civil Liberties Union
ACS - American Cancer Society
ACSI - Association of Christian Schools International
ADL - Anti-defamation League of B'nai B'rith
AFDC - Aid to Families with Dependent Children
AFL - American Football League
AFL-CIO - American Federation of Labor and Congress of Industrial Organizations
AFT - American Federation of Teachers
AKA - "also known as" (sometimes written "a.k.a")
AMA - American Medical Association (physicians' group)
AMVETS - American Veterans of World War II
ANSI - American National Standards Institute
AP - The Associated Press
APO - Army Post Office
ARIA - Adult Reading Improvement Association
ASCAP - American Society of Composers, Authors, and Publishers
ASCII - American Standard for Computer Information Interchange
ASTHMA - A Society to Help the Morale of Asthmatics
AT&T - American Telephone and Telegraph Company
BASIC - Beginners' All-Purpose Symbolic Instruction Code (computer language)
BBB - Better Business Bureau
BBC - British Broadcasting Corporation
BMOC - "big man on campus" (slang for a popular male student)
BSA - Boy Scouts of America
CAD - computer assisted drawing or computer aided design
CARE - Cooperative for American Relief Everywhere (sometimes includes periods)
CBC - Canadian Broadcasting Corporation
CBS - Columbia Broadcasting System
CD - compact disc

CD-ROM - compact disc acting as a read-only memory device (computer term)

CDC - Centers for Disease Control

CIA - (U.S.) Central Intelligence Agency

CLASS - Christian Liberty Academy School System

CNN - Cable News Network

CPA - certified public accountant

CPR - cardio-pulmonary resuscitation

CPU - central processing unit (computer term)

CSI - Christian Schools International

DAR - Daughters of the American Revolution

DAV - Disabled American Veterans

DBA - "doing business as" (sometimes written "d.b.a.")

DOS - disk operating system (computer term)

EC - European Community

EEOC - Equal Employment Opportunity Commission

EEU - European Economic Union

EPA - (U.S.) Environmental Protection Agency

ERA - Equal Rights Amendment; or "earned run average" (baseball term)

FAA - Federal Aviation Administration

FDA - (U.S.) Food and Drug Administration

FDIC - Federal Deposit Insurance Corporation

FPO - Fleet Post Office (U.S. Navy)

GATT - General Agreement on Tariffs and Trade

Gestapo - *Geheime Staats Polizei* (Nazi secret police) [*uncommon foreign words should be italized; bolding added*]

GIGO - "garbage in, garbage out" (computer term)

GOP - "Grand Old Party" (Republican Party, sometimes written with periods)

HHS - (U.S. Department of) Health and Human Services

HUD - (U.S. Department of) Housing and Urban Development

IBM - International Business Machines (corporation)

ICBM - intercontinental ballistic missile

IMF - International Monetary Fund

IRA - individual retirement account (banking); or Irish Republican Army

IRS - (U.S.) Internal Revenue Service

ISBN - international standard book number (library cataloging system)

KB - kilobyte (one thousand bytes — computer term)

KKK - Ku Klux Klan

LAN - local area network (computer term)

LCD - liquid crystal display (electronics term)

LED - light-emitting diode (electronics terms)

MADD - Mothers Against Drunk Driving (often written with periods)

MB - megabyte (one million bytes — computer term)

MFN - most-favored nation (international trade status)

NAACP - National Association for the Advancement of Colored People

NARAL - National Abortion Rights Action League

NASA - National Aeronautics and Space Administration

NBA - National Basketball Association

NBC - National Broadcasting Company

NCAA - National Collegiate Athletic Association

NEA - National Education Association; or National Endowment for the Arts

NEH - National Endowment for the Humanities

NFL - National Football League

NHL - National Hockey League

NLRB - National Labor Relations Board

NOW - National Organization for Women
NPS - National Park Service
NRA - National Rifle Association
NRLA - National Right-to-Life Association
OCR - optical character recognition (computer term)
OPEC - Organization of Petroleum Exporting Countries
OSHA - (U.S.) Occupational Safety and Health Administration
POW - prisoner of war (sometimes written with periods)
RAM - random access memory (computer term)
RBI - runs batted in (baseball term)
ROM - read-only memory (computer term)
SADD - Students Against Drunk Driving (sometimes written with periods)
SALT - Strategic Arms Limitation Treaty
SDI - Strategic Defense Initiative
SPCA - Society for the Prevention of Cruelty to Animals (Humane Society)
START - Strategic Arms Reduction Treaty
SWAT - special weapons and tactical team (police commando unit)
UFO - unidentified flying object
UN - United Nations
UPI - United Press International
UPS - United Parcel Service
USPS - United States Postal Service
WCTU - Women's Christian Temperance Union
WHO - World Health Organization
WWI - World War I
WWII - World War II
WYSIWYG - "what you see is what you get" (computer term)
YMCA - formerly Young Men's Christian Association
YWCA - formerly Young Women's Christian Association
ZPG - zero population growth

Lesson Fifty

◆ *Practice with Abbreviations*

Review *Lessons 48* and *49*. Rewrite the following sentences, correcting errors with abbreviations. Assume that sentences marked with an asterisk (*) fall within the category of formal writing.

1.* Chris. Columbus discovered Amer. Oct. 12, 1492.

_____

_____

2. The package was sent C.O.D.

_____

_____

3. She was born in the U.S.

_____

_____

4. The flights were scheduled at 7 AM and 2 PM.

_____

_____

5. The current time in the state of VA. is 4 pm E.S.T.

_____

_____

6. Saint Louis, MO, is her home.

_____

_____

7.* Governor Guy Hunt was the first Republican gov. in Ala. since the Civil War.

_____

_____

8. Seven people received a P.H.D. at the graduation.

_____

_____

9. Thousands of illegal aliens enter the U.S.A. every year.

_____

_____

10.* We bought 2 gals. of milk and 3 lbs. of cheese.

_____

_____

11.* Tues. or Wed. is a good day to shop.

_____

_____

12.* On which St. do you live?

_____

_____

13. No shipping charge is due on merchandise mailed fob Detroit.

_____

_____

14.* Nebuchadnezzar conquered Jerusalem approximately BC 586.

_____

_____

15.* Doctor Gaines made house calls.

_____

16.* Chas. Smitherman lives in our neighborhood.

17. The temple in Jerusalem was destroyed in 70 a.d.

18. Ft. Worth, Tx., has preserved its stockyard.

19. The *Today* program begins at 6 A.M., C.S.T.

20. Is her degree a Bs. or a Ba.?

Write acronyms or abbreviations for the following:

1. Mothers Against Drunk Driving   _____
2. intensive care unit   _____
3. World Health Organization   _____
4. "what you see is what you get"   _____
5. American Bar Association   _____
6. zero population growth   _____
7. Cable News Network   _____
8. Federal Bureau of Investigation   _____
9. Federal National Mortgage Association   _____
10. master of ceremonies   _____
11. individual retirement account   _____
12. International Monetary Fund   _____
13. United Nations Educational, Scientific, and Cultural Organization _____
14. North Atlantic Treaty Organization   _____
15. National Football League   _____
16. earned run average   _____
17. National Association for the Advancement of Colored People _____
18. National Right-to-Life Association   _____
19. Association of Christian Schools International   _____
20. most-favored nation   _____

Lesson Fifty-one

◆ *Writing Numbers*

A **numeral** is word, letter, figure, or group of words that expresses a number. Numerals can be classified in several different ways: 1) *cardinal* or *ordinal*; 2) *Arabic* or *Roman*; 3) *name* or *figure*.

Examples:

Cardinal name: *six*	Ordinal name: *sixth*
Cardinal Arabic figure: *6*	Ordinal Arabic figure: *6th*
Cardinal Roman figure: *VI*	Ordinal Roman figure: *(none)*

Learn the following guidelines for use of numerals in writing.

Journalistic writing:

1. Use Arabic forms unless referring to the sequence of wars or personal sequence for people and animals. (*World War II, Pope John XXIII*)

2. Never begin a sentence with a *figure* unless it is a figure representing a year; otherwise, always use numeral *names* at the beginning of a sentence.

3. Unless some specific other rule applies, use cardinal and ordinal *names* for numerals from zero through ten. Use figures for numerals 11 and up, except to begin a sentence. This general rule applies even to the use of numerals in a series. (*The company owned one 12-apartment building, ten three-bedroom homes, and 12 100-unit motels.*)

4. When names of large numbers must be used, use a hyphen to connect a word ending in *-y* to another word; do not use commas between words that are part of a numeral name. (*forty-one; two thousand three hundred thirty-seven*)

5. Use numeral names in casual expressions. (*A thousand thanks! Thanks a million!*)

6. In proper names, use numeral figures or numeral names according to the preference of the organization. (*20th Century Fox, Big Ten, Super 8 Motels*)

7. When using ordinal numerals in military, political, or geographic designations, or in expressing sequence in forming names, use figures. (*2nd Congressional District, 1st Precinct, 6th Ward, 7th Fleet, 101st Airborne, seaman 1st class; 9th U.S. Circuit Court of Appeals*)

8. Here are some other examples of journalistic usage of numerals:
   - *a 6-year-old girl, the boy was 5 years old.*
   - *Act 2, Scene 3*
   - *DC-10 aircraft*
   - *a 7-2 court decision*
   - *the Senate voted 51–49 in favor of the bill*
   - *the Giants defeated the Dodgers 5–3*
   - *No. 2 choice*
   - *20 percent, 6 percent, 2.5 percent, 0.6 percent*
   - *a ratio of 5 to 1, a 5–1 ratio*
   - *a range of $2 million to $14 million (not: $2 to $14 million)*

- *1 cent, $1.98, $32,000, $6.7 million*
- *telephone number: (916) 555–1234*
- *temperatures: minus 3, zero, 72 degrees*

Creative or formal (nonscientific) writing:

1. Generally, spell out numeral *names* for all numerals consisting of *one* or *two words*, unless in expressing years or sections of a book. (*three; sixty; four thousand; 1,237,345; chapter 5; page 13; Lesson 24; A.D. 1517; 1000 B.C.*)

2. In a sentence containing several numerals—some having one or two words and some having more than two words—use *figures* for all. (*About 40 of the 127 students failed the test.*)

3. Do not begin a sentence with a figure. (Follow Journalistic Guideline No. 2 above).

4. In nonscientific prose, use *names* of *ordinal* numerals, not *figures*. (*second, eighty-first*), unless other forms are used in proper names by preference of the organization.

5. Use numeral names for numbered streets under one hundred. (*Second Avenue, Forty-second Street, Ninth Street*)

6. In names of large numbers, use a hyphen to connect a word ending in *-y* to another word; do not use commas between words that are part of a numeral name. (*forty-one; two thousand three hundred thirty-seven*)

7. Arabic forms are generally preferred. Roman forms may be used in referring to the sequence of wars, in outline headings, in designations of book or magazine volumes, in paragraph numbering, in referring to personal sequence for people and animals, or in other appropriate uses according to the preference of the writer.

8. (Other specific guidelines are given in the following lessons.)

   Write the correct form for the following:

	3	7	17	61
Cardinal name	_____	_____	_____	_____
Cardinal Arabic figure	_____	_____	_____	_____
Cardinal Roman figure	_____	_____	_____	_____
Ordinal name	_____	_____	_____	_____
Ordinal figure	_____	_____	_____	_____

Lesson Fifty-two

◆ Writing Numbers

Learn these additional rules and guidelines for writing numbers.

1. Except in formal prose (as noted in the previous lesson), when a street name is a numeral, use ordinal names for streets numbered one through ten and ordinal figures for those above ten. (*First Street, Tenth Avenue, 17th Street*)

2. Do not use punctuation in postal zone codes, except for a hyphen in nine-digit U.S. ZIP Codes. (*Milaca, MN 56353; Grand Rapids, MI 49503; Oakdale, CA 95361-2045; Mississauga, ON L5G 4LS, Canada; 565 00 Mullsjö, Sweden*)

3. Do not use punctuation in house numbers or post office box numbers in addresses. (*3145 Maple St.; P.O. Box 2044*) However, a hyphen or dash may be used to avoid confusion by separating a house number from a numeric street name. (*123 – 27th St.*)

4. Do not put the conjunction *and* in a numeral name except when expressing a decimal point.

    Wrong: Four hundred *and* seventy-four

    Correct: Four hundred seventy-four

    Correct: Four hundred seventy-four *and* six tenths (474.6)

5. Fraction names are expressed in a combination of cardinals and ordinals, **without** a hyphen between the numerator and the denominator *if used as a noun*—unless either the numerator or denominator already has a hyphen. (*six tenths; ten thirty-seconds*)

NOTE: Fractions are *hyphenated*, however, if they are used as *adjectives* (e.g., a *two-thirds* vote of Congress; but as a *noun*, "*two thirds* of the congressional vote").

---

6. Mixed numbers, if not at the beginning of a sentence, are usually written with cardinal figures. (*The project cost 2 ½ times the original estimate.*)

7. Indefinite numbers should be written in cardinal names. (*About one hundred people attended.*)

8. Numbers over a million are usually written in a combination of cardinal figures and names. (*3 million; 345.6 billion; 3.5 trillion*)

    Write sentences containing numerals and illustrating each of the eight guidelines given in this lesson.

1. _____

   _____

2. _____

   _____

3. _____

   _____

4. _____

   _____

5. _____

   _____

6. _____

   _____

7. _____

   _____

8. _____

   _____

Lesson Fifty-three

◆ *Writing Numbers*

Many rules for the use of *numerals* are based on the general principle that figures, rather than numerical words, are more readily comprehended by the reader, particularly in technical, scientific, or statistical matter. However, because words are the basic building blocks for written communications, numbers are usually spelled out in more formal prose. As one handbook notes, the practice of writing words for numbers or of using figures is not so much a matter of correctness or incorrectness; it is one of convention, custom, and style. For this reason, many organizations, corporations, agencies, educational institutions, and other entities in which much writing is done develop their own "**style manuals,**" setting forth preferred forms for all aspects of writing, including one of the most varied aspects—the writing of numbers. Style rules and guidelines often differ in the four major categories of writing: *journalistic, scientific/ technical, creative/formal,* and *business.* Of course, numerals are used in other applications as well, such as in filling out forms and applications, in statistical tables, and in personal notations, where formal guidelines and rules may not be useful. Nevertheless, it is good to study some standard forms in order to bring continuity to our communications as much as possible. That is why several lessons are devoted to this matter in this workbook.

Learn these additional guidelines for writing numbers.

1. **Time of day.** Do not use the word *o'clock* or the phrases *in the morning* or *in the evening* with the abbreviations *a.m.* and *p.m.* (*The clock showed the time to be 12:01 a.m. The program will begin at 7 o'clock in the evening.* **Not:** *10 o'clock a.m.* or *10 a.m. in the morning*)

2. **Dates.** Except in filling out forms or other very informal situations, do not use cardinal figures in writing dates. (*June 14, 1994 not 6-14-94 or 6/14/94*)

NOTE: Outside of the United States, dates are often written as: 14 June 1994.

---

   a. Use ordinal numerals if the day precedes the month: *sixth of May* or *6th of May.*

   b. Use cardinal figures if the month precedes the day: *May 6.*

   c. Use complete figures for years, unless the year has some well-known special significance. (*The drought of 1989 hurt farmers. The Spirit of '76 lives on for most Americans.*)

   d. There are several acceptable forms for referring to *decades* and *centuries.*

   • *During the 1800s, railroads began to cross the Midwest. (Avoid this form.)*
   • *During the eighteen hundreds, railroads began to cross the Midwest.*
   • *During the nineteenth century, railroads began to cross the Midwest.*
   • *Rebellion was the spirit of the age during the Roaring '20s.*
   • *Rebellion was the spirit of the age during the Roaring Twenties.*
   • *The '50s were years of growth and prosperity.*
   • *My dad likes to listen to music from the Fifties.*
   • *The 1960s gave rise to the sexual revolution.*

3. **Plural of numbers.** Except as noted in 2d above, use an apostrophe to show the plural of figures. (*There are four 8's in his telephone number.*) This rule is not followed in the most commonly used journalistic stylebooks. In most newspapers, the plural of figures is written without an apostrophe. (i.e., *1980s, temperatures in the low 90s;* This is the preferred form.)

4. **Measurements.** Use the following forms. (Do not abbreviate measurement terms.)

   - *Standard U.S. letter-size paper is 8 ½ by 11 inches.*
   - *The quarterback carried the ball 5 yards.*
   - *The package weighed 2 pounds 6 ounces.*
   - *I wouldn't touch that with a 10-foot pole.*
   - *He installed a ¾-inch pipe.*
   - *The fence measured 20 feet 4 inches.*
   - *We lived in Europe for 2 years 3 months.*

5. **Money.** When there is only **one** reference to money in a sentence use the cardinal Arabic figure and the word *cents* for amounts of U.S. money under one dollar. Use cardinal figures and the dollar sign ($) for amounts of one dollar or more. Use figures or a combination of figures and words for amounts over a million.

   - *Doughnuts cost 75 cents each.*
   - *A gallon of gasoline cost an average of $1.58 at full-service stations in 1993.*
   - *No souvenir was less than $10.*
   - *The Legislature adopted a budget of about $502.5 million.*
   - *The exact budget figure was $502,451,250.13.*

   When there are **two or more** references to money in a sentence, some being below a dollar and others being above a dollar, all amounts should be written with figures and dollar signs.

   - *In Nova Scotia in 1991, one doughnut cost $ .75 and a gallon of gasoline cost $2.75.*
   - *Their postcards were $ .98, $1.50, and $2 each.*

6. **Business.** Use figures for *part numbers, model numbers, serial numbers,* and *payment dates and periods.*

   - *The television was identified by serial number 432N.*
   - *I need part 39765P for my food processor.*
   - *The payments are due every 30 days for 2 years.*
   - *Paying before the 10th of the month may save you some interest charges.*

7. **Percentage.** Always use cardinal figures to express percentages, unless the numeral comes at the beginning of a sentence. For fractional percentages, place a zero (0) before a decimal point. Do not use the percentage symbol (%) in formal writing.

   - *Fifty percent of the registered voters did not cast ballots.*
   - *The survey has an error margin of 4 percent.*
   - *Interest rates fell by 0.6 percent last month.*

8. **Ages.** In writing ages as "stand-alone" parenthetical matter, always use cardinal Arabic figures. Otherwise, follow the usual rule for numbers—spell out *one* through *ten*, use figures for 11 and up. If age is given in both years and months, use only figures (*see Lesson 51*).

   - *Elaine Dugan, 87, was honored at a party at the Senior Citizens' Center.*
   - *Ronald Reagan, at the age of 73, was the oldest man ever elected U.S. President.*
   - *Most children start kindergarten when they are five years old.*
   - *Many children can speak in complete sentences by the time they are 1 year 4 months old.*

9. **Miscellaneous.** Use cardinal figures for book pages, units, sections, and chapters; for lines in poems or books; for speeds; for highway numbers; for room and apartment numbers; and for clothing sizes. (*page 5; line 16; pp. 12–16; 65 miles per hour; Interstate 15, Route 66, U.S. 10, Hwy. 99; El Rancho Motel, Room 4; Greenwood Arms, Apartment 16; dress size 12; shoe size 6 ½*)

Lesson Fifty-four

◆ *Practice with Writing Numbers*

Rewrite the following sentences, making any necessary corrections in the use of numbers according to the guidelines in the previous lessons.

1. 16 people came to my birthday party.

   _____

2. I ordered six feet and six inches of pipe.

   _____

3. He is twelve years and two months old.

   _____

4. 3 of the twenty chairs were broken.

   _____

5. I paid sixty cents for the pen and a dollar for the paper.

   _____

6. Her address is fifteen 6th Street.

   _____

7. Several 100 dollars were wasted.

   _____

8. We shall leave at 7 A.M. in the morning.

   _____

9. 6 o'clock A.M. is too early.

   _____

10. August seventeenth is his birthday.

    _____

11. She was born sometime during the '70s.

    _____

12. The recipe called for one and one-half cups of flour.

    _____

13. The animal weighed seventy lbs. and twelve ozs.

    _____

14. The celebration will be six of August.

    _____

15. At least fifty % of my time was wasted.

    _____

16. The longest broad jump in the contest was six feet and eight inches.

_____

17. Pay within ten days and receive a discount.

_____

18. The Zip code in Seneca, S.C., is 34,721.

_____

Lesson Fifty-five

◆ *Practice with Writing Abbreviations*

Rewrite the following sentences, making any necessary corrections in abbreviations, according to the rules you learned in previous lessons.

1. Doctor Stone conducted the interview.

_____

2. His birthday is in Novem.

_____

3. The program starts at 7 P.M.

_____

4. The game is to be played in TEX. this year.

_____

5. The temperature is 99° Fahr.

_____

6. My street address is 6,210 East 7th Strt.

_____

7. The package arrived in the afternoon at 2:00 PM.

_____

8. Pres. Carter's hometown was Plains, Geor.

_____

9. The Super Bowl starts at 4:00 pm, C.S.T.

_____

10. The weight was 2 lb. and 6 oz.

_____

11. Wednes. or Thur. would be a good day to practice.

_____

12. The Protestant Reformation is said to have begun in 1517 a.d.

_____

13. Reverend Briggs is our new pastor.

_____

14. Mister Waits is a c.p.a.

_____

15. The school offers BA degrees in journalism and advertising.

_____

16. The United States Dept. of Education has been controversial.

_____

17. Their son received his PHD in botany.

_____

18. The first Mon. in Sept. is Labor Day.

_____

19. My math. exam. will be on Tues.

_____

Lesson Fifty-six

◆ *Practice with Writing Numbers and Abbreviations*

Rewrite these sentences, making any necessary corrections in the use of numbers or abbreviations.

1. He lives in Apartment # Six.

_____

2. Doctors Rose and Gaines were family practitioners.

_____

3. At age fourteen, he was six ft. and five in. tall.

_____

4. All of his grades were As.

_____

5. After 4 and one-half months, the practice became more intense.

_____

6. Did you pay ninety cents or a dollar-fifty for the pen?

_____

7. Mr.'s Borden, Lee, and Coleman were the men who helped.

_____

8. I have received her mail 3 times.

_____

9. Here is the complete address: _____

    Forty Six South Fifth Circle   _____

    Det. Michigan 73,106+1801   _____

10. He lives in Fort Lauderdale, FLOR.

    _____

11. 1st. graders learn to count by twos and fours.

    _____

12. The 4th Thurs. in Nov. is Thanksgiving Day.

    _____

13. Several 100 pigeons roost on that roof.

    _____

14. 65% of the audience came from N.Y.

    _____

15. The other thirty-five % were 18- and 19-year-olds.

    _____

16. 100 days of air assaults brought mass destruction on enemy territory.

    _____

17. The cost of the war exceeded $50,000,000,000.

    _____

18. The temp. in the desert can exceed 50° Ctgde.

    _____

19. The Bible was translated from Hebrew to Greek in about BC 300-200.

    _____

    _____

20. The plane arrived at 2:00 PM this afternoon.

    _____

21. "There be 3 things which are too wonderful for me, yea, 4 things which I know not..." (Prvbs. 30:18).

    _____

    _____

22. If your payment is made by June ninth, you will receive a two % discount.

    _____

    _____

23. Payments are due every thirty days.

    _____

24. Pres. Nixon was the only United States pres. to resign.

_____

25. My birthday party was planned for 6:15 PM o'clock Fri. night, Septem. 12th.

_____

_____

26. Either a Bs or a Ba degree is within your reach.

_____

27. City speed limits are generally 25-35 MPH.

_____

28. The space was three sq. yds.

_____

29. He is thirteen years and six months old today.

_____

30. Lieutenant Colonel Oliver North became a controversial public figure in the 80s and 90s.

_____

_____

Lesson Fifty-seven

◆ *Word Meanings and Figurative Language*

Diction is a term that refers to *the choice of words for clearness, correctness, or effectiveness of expression.* Good writing should always express good diction. There are a number of language concepts you should learn to help you with good diction in your writing and to help you fully appreciate good literature (and distinguish good literature from bad literature).

1. Denotation and Connotation

When we speak of the *meaning* of words, we may be referring to either the *denotative* or *connotative meaning.* **Denotation** is the literal, "dictionary" meaning of the word. **Connotation** is the suggestive, implied, or associated meaning of the word. Many words have both kinds of meanings. For example, the denotative meaning of the word *home* is "a dwelling, a place to live." But the word *home* has many different connotations (family warmth or strife, household fragrances, loving or spiteful relationships, etc.) for different people, depending on their associations with their own homes. Writing should always, of course, be as clear and accurate as possible; but use of words and phrases that are rich in suggested or implied values will often enhance communication of ideas.

2. Direct and Simple Words

Using words rich in suggestive value does not mean that you should always look for complicated or obscure words, however. In nearly every case, the use of *stilted* or *pretentious* words will distract the reader, confuse the reader, or bring ridicule upon the writer. Say "barber shop" rather than "tonsorial parlor." "Thief" is almost always better than "purloiner." Don't say "emporium" when you mean "store." Everyone will understand "swimming pool," but few will know what you mean by "natatorium."

3. Concrete versus Abstract Words

Simple is not always the same as *general*, however. When choosing words, select those that have precise, **concrete meanings**. "Walk" is abstract; "amble," "saunter," "hobble" are concrete. "The man hiked down the mountain" is abstract; "The rescuer felt his way through the crags and boulders" is concrete. One pitfall here, however, is the overuse of "flowery" language, leading to the creation of what has been called "purple prose," the tell-tale sign of amateur writing.

4. Similes

Effective writing makes good use of *figures of speech*. A **simile** is a form of figurative speech in which two things are compared by using the words *like* or *as*. *The snow on our lawn looked like a blanket of goose down. Her voice was as piercing as a trumpet blast.* Try to avoid the pitfall, however, of using *trite* or *hackneyed* expressions, such as *busy as a bee, clear as crystal, cold as ice*.

5. Metaphors

Another common and effective figure of speech is the **metaphor**. A metaphor is a comparison of two things **without** the use of the words *like* or *as*. *His concern for his wife was her security blanket. Lord, You are my hiding place.*

6. Alliteration

Writing can generate interest and beauty if the writer properly uses the repetition of sounds or accented syllables. This device is called **alliteration**. *He mustered amazing military might. A threatening throng approached the brick barricade.*

7. Direct Address and Personification

Occasional and appropriate use of **direct address** can be effective in making a literary point. Words used in direct address should be set off with commas. *Mr. Gorbachev, tear down this wall (Ronald Reagan). Please, Mr. Raindrop, keep falling on my garden.*

In some circumstances, objects or non-personal abstractions may be addressed or described as if they were persons. This device is known as **personification**. *The trees of the field will clap their hands.*

8. Irony

The use of humor, light sarcasm, or ridicule to imply meanings the opposite of what the chosen words literally state is called **irony**. *Going to the dentist is great fun; getting shots is even more enjoyable. "I found your discourse very stimulating," he yawned.*

9. Satire

Satire is a literary style often confused with *irony*. While irony may be used in satire, satire itself is literary composition that holds up human vices, shortcomings, abuses, or follies to ridicule, often with good-natured or humorous intent or intent to bring about improvement.

> By 1939 there were one hundred and seventy-three digests, or short cuts, in America, and even if a man read nothing but digests of selected material, and read continuously, he couldn't keep up. It was obvious that something more concentrated than digests would have to come along to take up the slack.
>
> It did. Someone conceived the idea of digesting the digests. He brought out a little publication called *Pith*, no bigger than your thumb.... It was not until 1960, when a ... graduate student named Abe Shapiro stepped in with an immense ingenious formula.... He was positive that he could take everything that was written and published each day, and reduce it to a six-letter word.

E.B. White, "Irtnog," from *Quo Vadimus*, 1935

10. Hyperbole

Hyperbole is gross exaggeration to produce a literary or rhetorical effect. It is obvious exaggeration with an emphasis that is not intended to be taken literally. *I was so parched I could have drunk a riverful of water. An aged man—easily twice as old as Methuselah—stood on the dock, gazing out into the sea.*

11. Metonymy

Metonymy is the use of one word to suggest another word or idea with which the selected word is associated or of which the selected word is reminiscent. *They took issue with **City Hall**. He has a reputation for chasing **skirts**. Limiting one's diet to **the garden** for a week will likely have a slimming effect.*

12. Litotes

Litotes make a point by denying the opposite. *The thunder was no light roar. The fire was no small blaze.*

13. Onomatopoeia

The use of a word whose very sound suggests its meaning is called **onomatopoeia**: *whoosh, buzz, fizz, splash, whistle, whine, squeal.*

14. Oxymorons

An **oxymoron** is a combination of two contradictory words. *His **thundering silence** gave everyone concern. Their son was a **holy terror**. He was a **communist entrepreneur**.*

15. Anachronisms

An **anachronism** is the rhetorical misplacement of an object, person, or event in an implausible or impossible setting or period of time. *Several television sets were arranged on the Round Table so that each of Arthur's knights could watch the football game without leaving their assigned seats. Antony and Cleopatra were quite the jet-setters.*

Write a sentence illustrating each of the following literary devices.

1. *simile*

    _____

    _____

2. *metaphor*

    _____

    _____

3. *hyperbole*

    _____

    _____

4. *alliteration*

    _____

    _____

5. *personification*

_____

_____

6. *onomatopoeia*

_____

_____

7. *anachronism*

_____

_____

Lesson Fifty-eight

◆ Spelling

Learn to pronounce and spell the following words.

1. extinction	7. athlete	13. periodically
2. endangered	8. punctuation	14. consumption
3. identifies	9. bibliography	15. distinguishing
4. additional	10. devastate	16. conservationist
5. appositive	11. tournament	17. introductory
6. ambition	12. publicity	18. campaign

Lesson Fifty-nine

◆ Spelling and Vocabulary

Learn to pronounce, spell, and identify the following words.

1. predator	7. practitioner	13. unsightly
2. glitch	8. scrutiny	14. vulture
3. condor	9. depredate	15. cyanide
4. adjacent	10. ingenuity	16. carrion
5. gerund	11. evoke	17. complement
6. infinitive	12. ornithologist	

Lesson Sixty

◆ *Vocabulary*

Fill in the blanks in the following sentences with appropriate words from *Lesson 59*.

1. Hearing a favorite old song would often _____ fond memories for my grandmother.

2. A _____ in the computer program caused valuable data to be lost.

3. The presence of _____ in their habitat area is important to the survival of scavenging birds and animals.

4. An _____ is a verb usually preceded by the introductory word *to*.

5. A _____ is an animal, bird, or person who preys upon others.

6. _____ poisoning intended for predators may inadvertently also kill valuable species.

7. A verbal ending in *-ing* and used as a noun is called a _____.

8. An _____ is a scientist trained in the zoology of birds.

9. A _____ is a very large vulture found in the Andes and in California.

10. The common _____ has often been called a buzzard.

11. Skill in developing a plan of action is called _____.

12. Any person practicing a given profession is called a _____.

13. My next-door neighbor and I live in _____ houses.

14. A close _____ of the problem revealed some errors.

15. Carrion, though food for vultures, is considered _____ and unhealthy by humans and is usually quickly removed from roadsides.

16. Good stewardship demands that we carefully manage activities that _____ natural resources.

17. Something that fills up or completes is a _____.

Lesson Sixty-one

◆ *Objective Complements*

Complements are words in a sentence that complete the meaning of thoughts begun by the subject and verb. Complements that refer to the subject of the sentence are called ***subjective complements***. Subjective complements include the following:

1. **predicate adjective** — an adjective that completes the thought begun by a linking verb by modifying the verb's subject.

2. **predicate nominative** — a substantive (noun, pronoun, or equivalent) that completes the thought begun by a linking verb by renaming or identifying the subject.

Complements that relate to the action of transitive verbs are called *objects*. They include the following:

1. **direct object** — a substantive that receives the action of a transitive verb.

2. **indirect object** — a substantive that tells *to whom/what* or *for whom/what* the action of a transitive verb is done.

A fifth type of complement is a word or group of words that *complete the meaning of objects*. Such a word or word group is called an **objective complement**—a noun, adjective, or the equivalent of either that is sometimes needed to complete the identity of a direct object.

This lesson is dedicated to the study of *objective complements*. In normal sentence order, they usually follow the direct object. If the objective complement is a substantive, it will rename or explain the direct object. If it is an adjective, it will modify the direct object. Objective complements usually follow verbs such as *make, think, consider, choose, elect, appoint, find, leave,* and *render*. A good way to identify an objective complement is to insert the phrase *to be* between the direct object and the word you wish to test. If *to be* fits logically, the second word is probably an objective complement.

Examples: Americans elected George Washington their first *President*.
We did not mean to leave you *defenseless*.
The verdict rendered the defendant *penniless*.
That makes me *angry*.
They chose Jeff *captain* of their team.

You have now studied the following basic patterns for simple sentences:

	Key
S.	= subject
I.V.	= intransitive verb
T.V.	= transitive verb
D.O.	= direct object
I.O.	= indirect object
O.C.	= objective complement
L.V.	= linking verb
P.N.	= predicate nominative
P.A.	= predicate adjective

S. ⇨ *I.V.* ◄———————————————————
A.   The *baby cried.*

S.   ⇨ *T.V.*   ⇨ *D.O.*
B.   *Mother calmed* the *baby.*

S. ⇨ *T.V.* ⇨ *I.O.*   ⇨ *D.O.*
C.   *Mother gave* the *baby* her *bottle.*

S.   ⇨ *T.V.*   ⇨ *D.O.* ⇨ *O.C.*
D.   *Everyone considered* the *baby contented.*

S. ⇨ *L.V.* ⇨*P.N.*
E.   The *baby was* a *girl.*

S. ⇨ *L.V.* ⇨ *P.A.*
F.   The *baby seemed satisfied.*

Write sentences using any form of these verbs, followed by *objective complements*.

1. *make*

_____

_____

2. *elect*

_____

_____

3. *name*

_____

_____

4. *find*

_____

_____

Lesson Sixty-two

◆ Appositives

An **appositive** is a substantive (noun, noun phrase, noun clause, gerund, gerundial phrase, infinitive, or infinitive phrase) added to (usually following) another noun or pronoun to further identify or explain it. The appositive signifies the same thing as the noun or pronoun it seeks to identify or explain.

Punctuating appositives:

1. Generally, enclose appositives with commas.

2. Omit the commas if the appositive is *restrictive (essential to meaning), part of a proper name, a single word,* or *closely related to the preceding word.*

3. Appositives with internal punctuation should be enclosed with dashes (—).

4. Some appositives are introduced by words such as *namely, for example, for instance, such as, i.e., e.g.,* etc. When this is so, place a comma after the introductory word.

Examples: His brother *Michael* was the key player in the tournament.

Michael, *his brother,* was the key player in the tournament.

Robert Louis Stevenson, *one of England's most beloved poets,* died in the South Pacific. (*noun phrase*)

America's major professional sports—*football, basketball, and baseball*—offer many athletes excellent income. (*internal punctuation*)

The politician's concession, *to release his personal financial records,* was prompted by his opponent's criticism. (*infinitive phrase*)

The fact *that I am a Christian* should not alarm you. (*restrictive noun clause*)

My ambition, *that I would make the Olympic team,* became a reality. (*nonrestrictive noun clause*)

Her only vice, *eating too much ice cream,* was taking its toll on her figure. (*gerundial phrase*)

Distinguishing between *adjective clauses* and *appositives* requires some scrutiny. An **adjective clause** *adds additional information* to the noun or pronoun it modifies. An **appositive** *restates* or *identifies* the noun or pronoun to which it refers.

Adjective Clause:

The Pan-American Games, *which were held in Cuba in 1991,* gave Cuba some worldwide publicity.

Appositive:

The Pan-American Games, *a much-publicized event,* involves athletes from throughout the Western Hemisphere.

Underline and *punctuate* the appositives and adjective clauses in the following sentences. In the blanks, indicate whether the appositive is a *noun, noun phrase, noun clause, gerund phrase,* or *infinitive phrase.* If the sentence contains an adjective clause, write *adjective clause* in the blank.

1. Only two species of condors the California condor and the Andean condor are in existence today. _____

2. The California condor's possible extinction a subject of much debate led to their declaration as endangered species. _____

3. By 1983, their total known population only 22 birds was said to be dangerously low. _____

4. A crisis in 1985 the death of six condors stirred more preservation action. _____

5. The desire of wildlife officials that the condors be saved brought strong support from conservationists. _____

6. The action of the government capturing the remaining condors required ingenuity. _____

7. Several alleged threats hunters, poisoning, and industrial development were cited as problems for the condors. _____

8. Lloyd Kiff an ornithologist led the California condor recovery team. _____

9. The team's decision to breed condors in captivity was questioned by some. _____

10. Two breeding places the Los Angeles Zoo and the San Diego Wild Animal Park were chosen for the project. _____

11. The cost more than $10 million will always be debated. _____

12. The breeding program a success story resulted in the birth of 13 chicks in 1991. _____

13. The desire of the recovery team that the chicks gradually be released into the wild became a reality in 1991. _____

14. The condor which belongs to the vulture family charms its admirers with its majestic soaring. _____

15. Its wings which have a spread of 8 to 11 feet rarely flap while the bird gracefully sails through the air. _____

Lesson Sixty-three

◆ *Practice with Appositives*

Write sentences with the following kinds of appositives. Punctuate the appositives properly.

1. *noun*

   _____

   _____

2. *infinitive phrase*

   _____

   _____

3. *gerundial phrase*

   _____

   _____

4. *appositive with internal commas*

   _____

   _____

5. *noun clause*

   _____

   _____

Lesson Sixty-four

◆ *Noun Clauses*

Noun clauses are dependent clauses that are used in a sentence in the same way single nouns are used. The six ways a noun or noun clause may be used are:

1. subject
2. direct object
3. indirect object
4. object of a preposition
5. predicate nominative
6. appositive

Noun clauses are introduced by *signal words* that connect them to the remainder of the sentence. Here are the most common *noun clause signal words*. Write and learn them.

1. what _____

2. whatever _____

3. who _____

4. whoever _____

5. that _____

6. where _____

7. wherever _____

8. when _____

9. whenever _____

10. whether _____

11. why _____

12. if _____

13. whom _____

14. whomever _____

15. which _____

16. whichever _____

17. how _____

18. however _____

Examples: *Noun clause as*:

Subject:

What you don't know may harm you.

Direct Object:

You have never told me *why you left so suddenly.*

Indirect Object:

He gave *whoever wanted one* a free copy of his book.

Object of a Preposition:

I can tell by *how you speak* that you are from the South.

Predicate nominative:

Things were not *what they seemed to be.*

Appositive:

His wish, *that he could go to Disneyland,* was finally fulfilled.

Lesson Sixty-five

◆ *Noun Clauses*

Underline the *noun clauses* in the following sentences. In the blank, tell how each is used. Some sentences may have more than one noun clause. Be careful not to confuse other dependent clauses for noun clauses.

1. That she was the daughter of nobility was clear from her mannerism. _____

2. The fact that you helped me when I was in dire need will never be forgotten.

   _____

3. Credit should go to whoever planned this fine celebration. _____

4. We do not know whether this plan will work. _____

5. The judge will give whoever vandalizes this property a stiff penalty. _____

6. With what the government now knows about them, many people do not feel secure in their own homes. _____

7. When more rain may come is hard to predict. _____

8. The wisdom of your suggestions may become apparent by how they work.

   _____

9. Some will continue to ask the question whether the war was worth the price.

   _____

10. Whatever one generation learns, another may forget. _____

11. Our desire is that the present generation will be more protective of its heritage.

    _____

12. Only time will tell if that is true. _____

13. What we hope is that it will be true. _____

14. Whether it becomes true depends on how each of us takes responsibility.

    _____

Lesson Sixty-six

◆ *Practice with Noun Clauses*

Write two sentences with noun clauses used in each of the six different ways nouns may be used. Underline the noun clauses.

Subject:

1. _____

2. _____

Direct Object:

1. _____

2. _____

Indirect Object:

1. _____

2. _____

Object of a Preposition:

1. _____

2. _____

Predicate Nominative:

1. _____

2. _____

Appositive:

1. _____

2. _____

Lesson Sixty-seven

◆ *Research Paper*

By now you should have made significant progress on the ***research paper*** you began in *Lesson 30*. Here is a checklist to measure your progress. You should have completed the first five steps at this point in your project. You should now begin writing your first draft, if you have not done so already.

❑ 1. Choose and limit your subject.

❑ 2. Find source material, prepare a working bibliography, and investigate your subject.

❑ 3. Prepare a preliminary outline.

❑ 4. Read and take notes.

❑ 5. Organize your notes and revise the outline as necessary.

❑ 6. Write a first draft of your paper, including footnotes.

❑ 7. Review and rewrite your first draft.

❑ 8. Edit your second draft.

❑ 9. Type and proofread your final paper.

Lesson Sixty-eight

◆ *Spelling*

1. managerial	9. suggestion	17. monologue
2. excel	10. notation	18. devastation
3. participle	11. explicitly	19. compliance
4. imperative	12. Hawaii	20. recommendation
5. evacuation	13. subjunctive	21. professional
6. occupation	14. indentation	22. negotiation
7. indicative	15. circumstantial	23. inauguration
8. mystique	16. humanitarian	24. confiscate

Lesson Sixty-nine

◆ *Spelling and Vocabulary*

Learn to pronounce, spell, and define the following words.

1. monarchy	7. incentive	13. parliamentary
2. kiosk	8. eclipse	14. independent
3. espouse	9. imperative	15. memorabilia
4. relics	10. diversity	16. aromatic
5. innate	11. vendor	17. medicinal
6. herb	12. noticeable	

Lesson Seventy

◆ *Vocabulary*

Write the words in *Lesson 69* in the blanks below where they fit best.

1. The _____ was displaying his merchandise.

2. Even though Christians have a _____ of spiritual gifts, they are expected to be unified in love and purpose.

3. Substances with _____ traits are used to reduce pain and cure diseases.

4. The magazine vendor sold his wares from a small _____ on the street corner.

5. Her _____ ability for music was apparent even though she had had few lessons.

6. Grandfather kept _____ from his war years in an old trunk in the attic.

7. It is _____ that you obey orders without question.

8. _____ is government or rule by one person.

9. We should not be forced to _____ ideas that violate our consciences.

10. The roses were especially _____, filling the room with a soft fragrance.

11. The rebellious teenager could not wait for the day she would be _____ from her parents' influence.

12. The sponsors offered a door prize as an _____ for attending the function.

13. Her _____ garden included basil, parsley, rosemary, and thyme.

14. Wooden ships are _____ of a bygone era of warfare.

15. Meetings conducted by proper _____ procedure usually are more orderly than informal discussions.

16. He had a _____ birthmark on his forehead.

17. A total _____ occurs when one celestial body completely obscures another.

Lesson Seventy-one

◆ Verbs

Perhaps the most noticeable errors in grammar come in the use of **verbs**. The next five lessons review the basic principles of verb use and structure.

Verbs have **four principal parts**: *present, past, past participle,* and *present participle.* Among the distinguishing characteristics are the fact that the second principal part never has a helping verb, the third principal part always has a helping verb (a form of the verb *have*) when used as part of a predicate, and the fourth principal part always ends in *-ing.*

Examples:

Present:	Past:	Past participle:	Present participle:
form	formed	(have, has, had) formed	forming
have, has	had	(have, has, had) had	having
bite	bit	(have, has, had) bitten	biting
soar	soared	(have, has, had) soared	soaring
be, is, are	was	(have, has, had) been	being
deserve	deserved	(have, has, had) deserved	deserving

Helping verbs are verbs that assist other verbs in forming voices, tenses, and other grammatical ideas. The most common are forms of *be, have, do, can, could, may, might, shall, should, will, would, must, ought, let, dare, need,* and *used.*

In the blanks, write the form of the verb needed in the sentence. If the verb has a helping verb, underline (___) it. (Do not supply any helping verbs that are not already printed in the sentences.) Double-underline (___) the subject of the sentence.

Example: Crayolas have (*give*) enjoyment to several generations. **given**

1. Students from former communist countries have (*take*) courses for managerial occupations in the United States. _____

2. In a few short months, Russia (*go*) from embracing communism to espousing democracy. _____

3. Czar Nicholas II, the last ruling monarch in Russia, was (*slay*) in 1918. _____

4. Memorabilia of the czar has (*begin*) to appear at street kiosks. _____

5. The old monarchy had once (*be*) a kind of religion in Russia. _____

6. Homemakers had (*hide*) relics of the czars for decades. _____

7. Communism has (*prove*) to be an utter failure. _____

8. During its time in Russia, it never (*give*) men any incentive to excel. _____

9. Innate skills (*lie*) dormant for a lifetime while communism was in force. _____

10. Christians (*go*) underground during the darkest years of persecution. _____

11. Occupations and professions were (*choose*) by the government. _____

12. Russian citizens have (*know*) about their distant past through well-preserved history books. _____

13. The last decade of the 20th century (*see*) the fall of the Berlin Wall. _____

14. The Berlin Wall had (*become*) a symbol of communism. _____

15. The Western world rejoiced that it had (*fall*). _____

Lesson Seventy-two

◆ *Tense and Tone of Verbs*

TENSE

Verbs have *tense.* Tense is the form that a verb takes to express the time of its action. The three simple tenses are *present, past,* and *future.* Verbs also have three perfect tenses: *present perfect, past perfect,* and *future perfect.* The perfect tenses are formed by using a form of the helping verb *have* followed by the past participle form of the main verb.

Examples:

Present:	Past:	Future:	Present perfect:	Past perfect:	Future perfect:
eat	ate	will eat	have/has eaten	had eaten	will have eaten
run	ran	will run	have/has run	had run	will have run
excel	excelled	will excel	have/has excelled	had excelled	will have excelled
rule	ruled	will rule	have/has ruled	had ruled	will have ruled
lie	lay	will lay	have/has lain	had lain	will have lain
lay	laid	will lay	have/has laid	had laid	will have laid
lie	lied	will lie	have/has lied	had lied	will have lied
write	wrote	will write	have/has written	had written	will have written
fall	fell	will fall	have/has fallen	had fallen	will have fallen

Use the correct tense to express time precisely.

1. **Present tense** expresses action or condition *now.*

2. **Past tense** expresses action or condition *before now.*

3. **Future tense** expresses action or condition *after now.*

4. **Present perfect tense** expresses action or condition that *began in the past and has just been completed or is still going on now.*

5. **Past perfect tense** expresses action or condition that *began in the past and was completed in the past.*

6. **Future perfect tense** expresses action or condition that *began in the past or is beginning now and will be completed at some future time.*

The *present tense* should also be used to express a timeless or universal truth. In a dependent clause, the *present tense* is used for this purpose even if the tense of the independent clause is in a different tense.

Example: In the past, it was not known that the earth is round.

In on-going prose, guard against *unnecessary* shifts in tense. All shifts should be logical and necessary.

Wrong: During summer vacation, we *traveled* to the Black Hills. Here we *visit* Mount Rushmore and *enjoy* camping at Custer State Park. In the evening, we *would sit* around the campfire.

Logical: While touring the Black Hills, we *visited* many historical sites. Some of the buildings in Deadwood ~~were~~ *are* very old. [*The buildings have not stopped being old; they are still old.*]

Be consistent in the selection of tenses of verbs in dependent and independent clauses. Follow proper sequence (the order of events in time).

• When the tense in the independent clause is *present, future, present perfect* or *future perfect*, any tense that adequately expresses the thought can be used in the dependent clause.

Examples: He *claims* that he *did* not *hit* his brother.
She *promises* that she *will come* to your party.

- When the tense in the independent clause is *past* or *past perfect*, the verb in the dependent clause should be in the *past* or *past perfect* tense, unless a timeless, general, or universal truth is being expressed in the dependent clause.

Examples: He *told* me he *saw* you at church yesterday.

She *heard* you say you *had been* in church.

They *said* they ~~will~~ *would come* to church next week.

- When actions in the past are told in the order in which they occurred, both verbs should be in the *past* tense. If the order is reversed, the action farther in the past should be in the *past perfect tense.*

Examples: The teacher *dismissed* the class, and the students *left* the room.

The students *left* the room after the teacher *had dismissed* the class.

TONE

Within some tenses, verbs also have **tone**. There are three verb tones: *simple, progressive,* and *emphatic.*

The **simple tone** is the common sense of the verb, a *concise, direct statement of the action or condition* being expressed (*study, sing, run, shout, cry,* etc.) in *any of the tenses.*

The **progressive tone**, sometimes referred to as a tense, expresses *continuing action or condition* (*am studying, are singing, is running, was shouting, will be crying, shall/will be eating, have/has/had been seeing, shall/will have been jumping,* etc.). *Active voice* verbs in progressive tone always end in *-ing* (present participle form) and are preceded by the proper tense forms of the helping verb *be* (see examples in previous sentence). In *passive voice,* the progressive form consists of a form of the helping verb *be,* followed by the present participle form of the verb *be* plus the past participle form of the main verb (*am being seen, were being seen,* etc.). In *active voice,* progressive tone occurs in *all six tenses.* In *passive voice,* it occurs only in the *present, past,* and *future tenses.*

The **emphatic tone** is used to *emphasize a statement* or *ask a question.* It is used only in the *present* and *past tenses* in *active voice.* (I *do study,* he *did sing,* she *does run,* Do they *shout?* Did she *cry?*) Emphatic tone uses the present infinitive (first principal part) form of the verb (without the *to*), preceded by the present or past form of the helping word *do.*

Write sentences using verbs of your choice in the tenses and tones indicated below. Underline the verbs, including any helping verbs. Some sentences, as indicated, will require two verbs. In such cases, place each in a separate clause. Use the simple tone unless otherwise specified. Use active voice only.

1. *present progressive*

   _____

   _____

2. *past and past perfect*

   _____

   _____

3. *future*

   _____

   _____

4. *present perfect*

_____

_____

5. *future perfect*

_____

_____

6. *present progressive*

_____

_____

7. *past emphatic*

_____

_____

8. *future perfect progressive*

_____

_____

9. *present emphatic*

_____

_____

10. *past progressive*

_____

_____

11. *future perfect*

_____

_____

12. *past perfect progressive*

_____

_____

Lesson Seventy-three

◆ *Voice of Verbs*

Verbs have **voice**. If the doer of the action is the subject, the voice of the verb is *active*. If the doer of the action (named or unnamed) is *not* the subject, the verb is in *passive voice*.

Generally, **active voice** is preferred and makes writing stronger. However, passive voice may be used effectively for variety. It may be used when the doer of the action *is not known* to the writer or *is obvious* to the reader. Passive voice may be used when the writer wishes to express his or her thoughts in an *impersonal* manner by merely implying or deliberately not naming the identity of the doer of the action.

If the doer of the action is not named in a passive-voice sentence, the sentence cannot be rewritten into active voice. Intransitive and linking verbs cannot be written in passive voice.

Rewrite the following sentences, changing the voice of the verb from active to passive or from passive to active. Maintain the tense and tone of the original sentence.

Example: A total eclipse of the sun was seen by residents of Hawaii in 1991.
      Residents of Hawaii saw a total eclipse of the sun in 1991.

1. A leap from a plane was planned by 30 skydivers.

   _____

2. The site was crowded with 5,000 concertgoers.

   _____

3. Tourists spent $15 million at the exposition.

   _____

4. Officials tallied receipts from the fund-raiser for several hours.

   _____

5. John changed this sentence from active to passive voice.

   _____

   _____

6. This sentence was changed by Mary from passive to active voice.

   _____

   _____

7. Mike was being given some money by his father.

   _____

   _____

8. The cake will have been eaten by the guests before you get here.

   _____

   _____

9. Microbes have never been seen by the naked eye.

   _____

   _____

10. He will be recognized by his peers at an awards banquet.

   _____

   _____

11. She sold the house within a month after its appearance on the market.

   _____

   _____

12. Edvard Grieg wrote the *Peer Gynt Suites*.

_____

_____

Lesson Seventy-four

◆ *Mood of Verbs*

Verbs have **mood** (sometimes called *mode*). *Mood* indicates the *state of mind* or *manner* in which a statement is made. English verbs have three moods: *indicative, imperative,* and *subjunctive.*

Indicative mood is used to state (indicate) a fact or to ask a question of fact. Most speaking and writing is done in the indicative mood.

Examples: Your research paper will soon be due.

Did you turn off the light?

Imperative mood is used to issue a command or express a request.

Examples: Please come to my party.

Stop! Do not pass this barrier!

Go to the store and buy a quart of milk.

Subjunctive mood is used to express a *wish, doubt, necessity, uncertainty, desire, supposition, improbable condition,* or *condition contrary to fact.*

The verb *to be* has only two subjunctive forms: 1) *be* for all persons (first, second, and third) in both the singular and plural present tense (no longer common in modern usage); and 2) *were* for all persons in the singular and plural past tense.

For all other verbs, the subjunctive form of verbs is the same as the form for the indicative mood—with one exception: *the third person singular present.* In this exception, the form used is the identical to the plural.

Examples: If this *be* your preference, I will order it. (*archaic; modern usage = "is"*)

If I *were* you, I would not do that.

If you *see* fit, send him one of your books.

He acts as though he *were* chairman of this committee.

It is necessary that she *pass* the test.

The President requested that the news media *be alerted.*

The requirement that all papers *be* properly *endorsed* was clearly stated.

The recommendation that we *be* cautious was wise.

The subjunctive mood is also used to express *parliamentary motions.*

Examples: I move that the committee *be authorized* to select its own chairman.

The motion was made that the comments of the witness *be stricken* from the record.

In expressing a condition contrary to fact, the dependent clause (usually an adverbial clause) will often begin with the subordinating conjunctions *if, as if,* or *as though.* In this case, the verb should be in the subjunctive mood. However, these same conjunctions may also be used in clauses expressed in the indicative mood when the clause is making a statement of fact. Be certain of the "state of mind" being expressed so that the correct *mood* of the verb is chosen.

Examples: If the hurricane *hits* land (and it may), damage will occur. (*indicative*)

If I *were* you (and I am not), I would not wait to evacuate. (*subjunctive*)

Although our language no longer makes great use of the subjunctive-mood forms, some common expresses are retained. Learn to recognize the following, for example:

Thy Kingdom come, Thy will be done   *heaven forbid*   *if need be*

come what may   *suffice it to say*   *he need not...*

In many instances, traditional subjunctive-mood forms of verbs have been replaced by the use of certain *auxiliary (helping) verbs* to express variations in "mood" or "state of mind." These include: *should, would, can, could, may, might, must, ought, let, dare, need, used.* Verb phrases using these helping verbs are considered to be in the subjunctive mood *if they express one of the states of mind for which subjunctive mood is used (condition, doubt, desire, necessity, etc.).* In other cases, these helping verbs may be used in the indicative mood.

Archaic: If he *come*, it will be wonderful.

If she *decide* to sing, I shall accompany her.

Current: If he *can come*, it will be wonderful.

If she *should decide* to sing, I shall accompany her.

Complete the following exercise by filling in the blanks.

Verbs have _____ moods. They are: _____

              (number)   _____

                                           _____

The *indicative mood* is used for the following purposes: _____

_____

The *imperative mood* is used for the following purposes: _____

_____

The *subjunctive mood* is used to express:

_____   _____   _____

_____   _____   _____

_____   _____

Look up the following passages in the King James Version of the Bible. Write any phrases or clauses you find there that have verbs in the subjunctive mood.

Genesis 8:8   _____

Genesis 27:46   _____

Genesis 42:38 _____

Exodus 22:3 _____

_____

Nehemiah 2:5 _____

_____

Job 14:7 _____

Psalm 11:3 _____

Psalm 50:12 _____

Prov. 6:30–31 _____

_____

Prov. 29:12 _____

Matt. 10:13 _____

_____

Mark 9:35 _____

Acts 25:11 _____

_____

I Cor. 3:17 _____

Phil. 4:8 _____

_____

Lesson Seventy-five

◆ *Mood of Verbs*

Underline (___) all subjects of the following sentences (including those in dependent clauses). Double-underline (___) all verbs. In the blanks, name the *mood* of the verbs you have double-underlined.

Example: My <u>friend</u> <u>wishes</u> <u>he</u> <u>were</u> a professional jockey.   1.   *indicative*
                                                                                                                  2.   *subjunctive*

1. _____ Read the directions carefully. _____

2. Soccer is not a major sport in the United States. _____

3. I wish the growing season in Alaska were longer.   1. _____

                                                                                             2. _____

4. Do hummingbirds migrate? _____

5. It is vital that the count be accurate.   1. _____

                                                     2. _____

6. The child performed as though he were a professional. 1. _____

                                                     2. _____

7. Many are recommending that the school year be lengthened.

                                                     1. _____

                                                     2. _____

8. _____ Follow the instructions explicitly. _____

9. The flood water covered a major highway in the area. _____

10. What is the widest wingspread of a condor? _____

11. A motion was made that the legislature be adjourned. 1. _____

                                                     2. _____

12. _____ Store all important records in fireproof containers. _____

13. If I were the queen, I would not enjoy the fanfare. 1. _____

                                                     2. _____

14. I doubt that the story be (is) true.   1. _____

                                                     2. _____

15. Every journalist should check his story for accuracy. _____

16. The animal wailed as though it were seriously hurt. 1. _____

                                                     2. _____

17. Which political party controls the legislature in your state? _____

18. She moved that the minutes of the meeting be approved.

                                                     1. _____

                                                     2. _____

Lesson Seventy-six

◆ Paragraphs

There are four primary types of writing or paragraph development. Name them and explain each. (See *Lesson 1* for review of these concepts.)

1. _____

2. _____

3. _____

4. _____

Explain the purpose of the topic sentence.

Choose a common or specialized task, such as an errand that you regularly perform within your home or a procedure you have learned at a part-time job. In a brief paragraph, explain how that task is performed. Keep the steps of procedure in proper sequence so that a reader can follow them and, if necessary, could perform the same task.

_____

_____

_____

_____

_____

_____

_____

_____

_____

_____

_____

_____

_____

_____

_____

_____

_____

_____

_____

Lesson Seventy-seven

◆ Spelling

Learn to pronounce and spell the following words.

1. compliance
2. instability
3. financially
4. knowledgeable
5. government
6. charitable
7. organization
8. volunteer
9. abbreviation
10. factual
11. policy
12. philosophy
13. executive
14. peculiarity
15. formula

Lesson Seventy-eight

◆ *Spelling and Vocabulary*

Learn to pronounce, spell, and identify the following words.

1. bureaucracy
2. correlative
3. chancellor
4. coup d'etat
5. ambivalence

6. capitalism
7. subservient
8. bolshevism
9. conspirator
10. regime

11. junta
12. resolute
13. Septuagint
14. irrevocably
15. synonymous

Lesson Seventy-nine

◆ *Vocabulary*

Fill in the blanks in the sentences below with words from *Lesson 78*.

1. The generals who led the revolution formed a _____ to rule until an election could be held.

2. The amount that could be withdrawn from the trust fund was _____ fixed by the wealthy man's will.

3. To be _____, two ideas must have the same meaning and implications.

4. _____ is an economic system characterized by private or corporate ownership and by competition in the marketplace.

5. A _____ is the whole body of non-elected officials serving in the administration of government.

6. A _____ is a violent effort to overthrow an existing government.

7. The _____ is a translation of the Old Testament from Hebrew to Greek.

8. _____ was a particular branch of the communist movement in Russia early in the twentieth century.

9. Every man who helped plan the coup d'etat was a _____.

10. An executive officer of some countries, schools, or courts is a _____.

11. A _____ position is one of lesser rank requiring submission to authority.

12. Words that are _____ are words that correspond or have a reciprocal relationship with each other.

13. He was _____ in his determination to obtain the job.

14. _____ in one's beliefs often leads to confusion and inability to defend one's actions.

15. A regular pattern of government or the period of time a given government rules is called a

_____.

Lesson Eighty

◆ *Argumentative Paragraph*

Choose a current social, economic, or political issue being publicly debated. Write a paragraph expressing your views. Give several reasons why you are sure your views are the correct ones. This type of writing is called _____.

_____

_____

_____

_____

_____

_____

_____

_____

_____

_____

_____

_____

_____

_____

_____

_____

_____

_____

_____

_____

_____

_____

_____

_____

_____
_____
_____
_____
_____
_____
_____

Lesson Eighty-one

◆ *Voice of Verbs*

What is meant by *voice* in the use of verbs?_____

_____

_____

Write five sentences using verbs in *active voice*.

1. _____

_____

2. _____

_____

3. _____

_____

4. _____

_____

5. _____

_____

Write five sentences using verbs in *passive voice*.

1. _____

_____

2. _____

_____

3. _____

_____

4. _____

_____

5. _____

_____

Lesson Eighty-two

◆ Mood of Verbs

In the following sentences, underline the verbs. In the blanks, tell the *mood* of the verbs you have underlined.

1. Have the people been happy with their lifestyle? _____

2. Listen to the radio for further word about the storm. _____

3. People in poor countries wish there were more food. 1. _____
                                                        2. _____

4. Were a farmer to own his own land, his incentive to produce would increase.
                                                        1. _____
                                                        2. _____

5. It became imperative that new policies be made.   1. _____
                                                        2. _____

6. The experiment was a failure. _____

7. Watch for social instability as political changes occur. 1. _____
                                                        2. _____

8. Our country cannot be of much help financially. _____

9. It is important that the new president be knowledgeable.
                                                        1. _____
                                                        2. _____

10. The new rulers' ambivalence toward democracy was evident. _____

11. If I were in charge, I would adopt a new policy.   1. _____
                                                        2. _____

12. Had communism survived in the Soviet Union, millions would still be in bondage.
                                                        1. _____
                                                        2. _____

Lesson Eighty-three

◆ Subject-Verb Agreement

Review *Lessons 9, 10, 15,* and *16.* Write a sentence illustrating each of the following rules for subject-verb agreement.

1. When the subject of a sentence is an indefinite pronoun such as *most, some, few,* etc., the pronoun's antecedent (which is usually the object of a prepositional phrase following the subject) determines its number and the number of the verb.

_____

_____

2. When the subject of a sentence is a *fraction*, its number and that of the verb are also determined by the fraction's antecedent.

_____

_____

3. When the word *number* is the subject of a sentence, it is singular if preceded by the article *the*.

_____

_____

4. When the word *number* is the subject of a sentence, it is plural if preceded by the article *a*.

_____

_____

5. Compound subjects usually require a plural verb.

_____

_____

6. Compound subjects preceded by the word *each* require a singular verb.

_____

_____

7. Compound subjects preceded by the word *every* require a singular verb.

_____

_____

8. Compound subjects that refer to one and the same entity require a singular verb.

_____

_____

9. When two singular subjects are connected by *either...or* or *neither...nor*, the verb must be singular.

_____

_____

10. When two plural subjects are connected by *either...or* or *neither...nor*, the verb must be plural.

_____

_____

11. When a singular subject and a plural subject are connected by *either...or* or *neither...nor*, the one nearest the verb determines the number of the verb.

_____

_____

12. The number of the verb in an adjective clause is determined by the *antecedent* of the relative pronoun that introduces the clause.

_____

_____

13. When a subject is followed by a phrase introduced by such expressions as *together with, as well as, along with*, etc., the number of the verb in the sentence is not affected by the intervening phrase.

_____

_____

14. Subjects that are plural in form but singular in usage (amounts of money, weights, measurements, periods of time, etc.) require a singular verb.

_____

_____

Lesson Eighty-four

◆ *Subject-Verb Agreement*

Underline the verb that agrees with its subject in the following sentences.

1. Three of the men who (was, were) named to the committee were Republicans.

2. One of the men who (was, were) named to the committee was a Democrat.

3. Neither the U.S. President nor the leader of any other Western nation (has, have) expressed his views on the subject.

4. The secretary and treasurer of the garden club (give, gives) her report at each meeting.

5. The number of people supporting democracy (continue, continues) to grow.

6. A number of patriots (have given, has given) their lives for freedom.

7. An American tennis player, as well as players from Sweden and France, (are, is) favored to win the tournament.

8. Each of the reforms—whether they be political, social, or economic—(enhances, enhance) prospects for democracy.

9. Every man, woman, and child in America (is, are) responsible to help preserve freedom.

10. He or she who (vote, votes) (utilize, utilizes) one of the foundation stones of democracy.

11. Oftentimes, much of the money given to charities (go, goes) to administrative costs.

12. Half of the food items delivered for famine relief (was taken, were taken) by rebel soldiers.

13. Either charitable organizations from abroad or local volunteers (distribute, distributes) what actually reaches the hungry.

14. The hand that (rock, rocks) the cradle (rule, rules) the world.

Lesson Eighty-five

◆ *Narrative Paragraph*

Narrative writing tells a story. Recall a memorable incident from your childhood and write a narrative relating the story. Include some dialogue, if possible.

_____

_____

_____

_____

_____

_____

_____

_____

_____

_____

_____

_____

_____

_____

_____

_____

_____

_____

_____

_____

_____

_____

_____

_____

_____

Lesson Eighty-six

◆ *Elliptical Clauses*

Review *Lessons 41* and *42*. A dependent clause from which words have been omitted but are implied is called an _____ clause. For such a clause to be correctly written, the implied subject of the _____ clause and stated subject of the _____ clause must be the same or refer to the same thing.

Rewrite the following sentences, making one of the clauses an elliptical clause. If some of the sentences cannot be changed, explain why in the blanks.

1. When Tara was less than four years old, she lost her father.

   _____

   _____

2. Since Ray was an experienced mountain climber, his friends asked him to lead the expedition.

   _____

   _____

3. Gene and Mark reached the summit while they were climbing together.

   _____

   _____

4. Edward was the first to win the prize even though he was only 14 years old.

   _____

   _____

5. Though Mount McKinley is North America's tallest peak, it is not the highest mountain in the world.

   _____

   _____

6. While Lonny was eating his breakfast, the telephone rang.

   _____

   _____

7. While Lonny was eating his lunch, he heard the telephone ring again.

   _____

   _____

Lesson Eighty-seven

◆ Errors with Abbreviations

Review *Lessons 48* and *49*. Underline the abbreviations below that are in error. Write the correct forms in the blanks.

1. His birthday is on Thur. _____

2. Mr.'s Smith and Jones are candidates for the Senate. _____

3. The program begins at 6 P.M. _____

4. It is 5 o'clock, e.s.t., in the state of G.A. _____

5. The star player, Chas. Mason, was injured. _____

6. Pres. Harry Truman was a plain-spoken man. _____

7. Some aliens enter the U.S. illegally. _____

8. How long have you lived in Hartford, CT.? _____

9. We bought a gal. of ice cream. _____

10. The snake was six ft. long. _____

11. The speed limit is now 65 mi. per hr. _____

12. Nov. eleventh is Veterans Day. _____

13. Ronald Clanton, doctor of medicine, is the guest speaker. _____

14. Mrs.'s Ford, Reagan, and Bush were wives of presidents. _____

15. The Red River flows through Shreveport, L.A. _____

16. "Behold, I come quickly…" (Revel. 22:7). _____

17. Sergnt. York was a hero. _____

Lesson Eighty-eight

◆ Errors with Numbers

Numbers (and some associated words) are written incorrectly in the following sentences. Underline the errors and write corrections in the blanks.

1. The war lasted only forty three days. _____

2. The incorrect answers were twenty-three % of the total. _____

3. 35 contestants registered, and 9 were girls.   _____

4. The cost of the program was $fifty-billion.   _____

5. The town was decorated with 100's of yellow ribbons.   _____

6. Her shoe size increased to size seven.   _____

7. We arrived on 8-2-90.   _____

8. He boarded a bus to leave at 3:15 P.M. o'clock.   _____

9. His oldest son was twelve years and six months old.   _____

10. They each needed ninety cents for their lunch.   _____

Lesson Eighty-nine

◆ *General Errors*

Every sentence below contains at least one error. Some have more than one. Rewrite the sentences, correcting the errors.

1. 65 people attended the meeting.

    _____

2. As soon as the rain came the temperature dropped.

    _____

3. I wish I was you.

    _____

4. Every one of the republics want independence.

    _____

5. The boat, along with the motor, sell for $1,000.

    _____

6. Books cost ten dollars, pens seventy-five cents, and notebooks one dollar and twenty-five cents.

    _____

    _____

7. The plant's address is Rural Route Nmbr. Six.

    _____

8. My brother is five feet and nine inches tall.

    _____

9. School starts in Aug. or Sept.

    _____

10. The artifacts dated from BC 200.

   _____

11. On my thirteenth birthday, I weighed eighty-five lbs. and fourteen oz.

   _____

12. He graduated from college in '89.

   _____

13. He spent 2/3 of his time in China.

   _____

14. It is urgent that she meets all requirements for the contest.

   _____

15. One of the missiles which were not intercepted killed several civilians.

   _____

16. A number of countries was contributors to the cost of the program.

   _____

17. Money, along with military personnel, were needed.

   _____

18. The tomato, as well as the orange, contain vitamin C.

   _____

19. The trucks and the car has been moved.

   _____

20. Bob did not get much work done today, he received too many phone calls.

   _____

21. When eating lobster, a bib should be worn.

   _____

22. The two senators who each state elects represent their states at large.

   _____

Lesson Ninety

◆ *Descriptive Paragraph*

Write a descriptive paragraph about the person who has helped or influenced you the most during the past year.

   _____

   _____

   _____

   _____

Appendix

TABLE OF IRREGULAR VERBS

Present (to +)	Past	Past Participle (have, has, had+)	Present (to +)	Past	Past Participle (have, has, had+)
arise	arose	arisen	pay*	paid	paid
bear	bore	borne, born	prove	proved	proved, proven
beat	beat	beaten	put	put	put
become	became	become	rise	rose	risen
begin	began	begun	ride	rode	ridden
bid (auction)	bid	bid	ring	rang	rung
bid (command)	bade, bid	bidden, bid	run	ran	run
bite	bit	bitten	say*	said	said
blow	blew	blown	see	saw	seen
break	broke	broken	set	set	set
bring	brought	brought	sit	sat	sat
build	built	built	shine (gleam)**	shone	shone
burn	burned, burnt	burned, burnt	show	showed	shown, showed
burst	burst	burst	shrink	shrank, shrunk	shrunk
cast	cast	cast	sing	sang	sung
catch	caught	caught	sink	sank, sunk	sunk
choose	chose	chosen	sleep	slept	slept
come	came	come	speak	spoke	spoken
cut	cut	cut	spend	spent	spent
dig	dug	dug	spring	sprang, sprung	sprung
dive	dived, dove	dived	stand	stood	stood
do	did	done	steal	stole	stolen
draw	drew	drawn	swear	swore	sworn
drink	drank	drunk, drunken	swim	swam	swum
drive	drove	driven	swing	swung	swung
eat	ate	eaten	take	took	taken
fall	fell	fallen	tear	tore	torn
feel	felt	felt	think	thought	thought
find	found	found	throw	threw	thrown
flee	fled	fled	wake	waked, woke	waked, woken
fly (sail)**	flew	flown	wear	wore	worn
forecast	forecast, (-ed)	forecast, (-ed)	weep	wept	wept
forget	forgot	forgotten	win	won	won
freeze	froze	frozen	wind	wound	wound
get	got	got, gotten	wring	wrung	wrung
give	gave	given	write	wrote	written
go	went	gone			
grow	grew	grown			
hang (object)**	hung	hung			
know	knew	known			
lay*	laid	laid			
lead	led	led			
lend	lent	lent			
let	let	let			
lie (recline)**	lay	lain			
lose	lost	lost			
meet	met	met			

*lay, pay, and say may also be considered regular verbs in that they use the regular ending -d to form the past and past participle—after changing the final "y" to "i."

**Other meanings have regular parts:

fly (hit baseball)	flied	flied
lie (tell falsehood)	lied	lied
hang (by the neck)	hanged	hanged
shine (polish)	shined	shined

Glossary

Absolute phrase or **Absolute expression.** A noun or pronoun followed by a modifying participle, either expressed or understood. The expression is called "absolute" because it does not modify any specific word in the sentence, yet it usually cannot stand alone in a sentence.

    Examples: *The men having finished their work,* the foremen sent them home. The meeting began, *the preliminary social hour (being) over.*

Absolutes. Adjectives and adverbs that are logically incapable of comparison because their meanings are absolute. Such words include: *unique, perfect, perpendicular, horizontal, parallel, excellent, accurate, absolute, round, square, final, fatal, impossible, correct, current, normal, original, average.* Comparison may be achieved only by the addition of qualifying adverbs, such as *nearly, more/most nearly, almost.*

Active voice. The form of an action verb that tells that the subject is the doer of the action.

    Example: George *mowed* his lawn.

Adjective. A part of speech that modifies or limits the meaning of a noun or pronoun. They usually answer one of the following questions about the noun or pronoun they modify: *which one? what kind? how much? how many?* Simple adjectives are generally located immediately before the word they modify. Predicate adjectives are usually located after a linking verb and modify the subject of that verb.

    Examples: the *happy* people (*simple adjective*); The eggs are *rotten.* (*predicate adjective*)

Adjective clause. A dependent clause used to modify a noun or pronoun.

    Example: The car *which you rented* must be returned tomorrow.

Adverb. A part of speech that modifies a verb, adjective, or another adverb. Adverbs used as transitional devices in sentences may modify the entire thought of the sentence.

    Example: We are, *however,* planning to visit you shortly.

Adverb (adverbial) clause. A dependent clause that modifies a verb, adjective, or adverb.

    Examples: Mary quit her job *because she preferred her role as a mother.* (*modifies verb*)

    The test was harder *than most others were.* (*modifies adjective*)

    I think more sharply *after a good night's rest.* (*modifies adverb*)

Agreement. Sameness in number, gender, and person. Agreement in number is required between a subject and predicate. Pronouns must agree with their antecedents in person, number, and gender.

Antecedent. The substantive (*noun* or *pronoun*) to which a pronoun refers.

Appositive. A noun or noun clause added to (usually following) another noun or pronoun to further identify or explain it. The appositive signifies the same thing as the noun or pronoun it seeks to identify or explain.

    Examples: One economic system, *socialism,* is a proven failure.

    A basic socialist premise, *that all people deserve an equal share of the world's material substance,* is a false assumption.

Auxiliary verb. Also called a **helping verb**. A verb used to "help" another verb in forming voices, tenses, and other grammatical ideas. The most common are forms of *be, have, do, can, could, may, might, shall, should, will, would, must, ought, let, dare, need,* and *used.*

Case. The forms that nouns or pronouns have (*nominative, objective, possessive*) signifying their relationship to other words in a sentence.

Examples: The *car* was new. (*nominative*)

The subject of the *speech* was crime. (*objective*)

The *children's* story hour was always popular. (*possessive*)

Clause. A group of words including a subject and a predicate and forming a part of a sentence. All words in a sentence must be part of a clause. Clauses are classified as to their *use* (*adjective, adverb, noun*), their *character* (dependent, independent, elliptical), and their *necessity* (*essential* [restrictive], *non-essential* [non-restrictive]).

Clew. That portion of a topic sentence that gives "clues" as to what a paragraph is going to say about the subject or "topic" of the paragraph.

Comparative degree. The form of an adjective or adverb used when comparing two entities. The comparative form is created by adding *-er* to one-syllable and some two-syllable adjectives and adverbs or by preceding adjectives and adverbs of two or more syllables with the word *more.*

Examples: That painting is *prettier* than the other one.

Robert seems to learn *more easily* than Sally. (*See also Absolutes.*)

Comparison, degrees of. A change in the form of adjectives and adverbs signifying greater or smaller degrees of quantity, quality, or manner. The three degrees of comparison are: *positive, comparative,* and *superlative.*

Examples: *small, smaller, smallest; beautiful, more beautiful, most beautiful*

Complement. A word or expression used to *complete* the action or idea indicated by a verb. Predicate *complements* include predicate nominatives (*noun* or *pronoun*) and predicate adjectives following linking verbs and describing, identifying, or modifying the subject.

Complex sentence. A sentence consisting of one independent clause and one or more dependent clauses.

Example: When Jesus came, He preached a message of salvation to all who would believe.

Compound sentence. A sentence consisting of two or more independent clauses.

Example: The battle was won, but the war was lost.

Compound-complex sentence. A sentence consisting of two or more independent clauses and one or more dependent clauses.

Example: Since Mike was artistic, he designed the brochure; but Jennifer, who was a better writer, wrote the text.

Conjugation. Changes in the form and use of a verb to signify *tense, voice, number, person,* and *mood.*

Conjunction. A part of speech used to connect words or groups of words such as phrases and clauses. Conjunctions are classified as *coordinating* when they link equal elements or *subordinating* when they link unequal elements.

Examples: I like apples *and* bananas. (*coordinating conjunction linking two direct objects*)

My hair is brown, *whereas* Mary's is blonde. (*subordinating conjunction linking an independent clause with a dependent clause*) (*See also Conjunctive adverb.*)

Conjunctive adverb. An adverb used as a coordinating conjunction connecting two independent clauses.

> **Example:**   The picnic was cancelled; *nevertheless*, we had a pleasant afternoon in the park.

Coordinating conjunction. A conjunction linking words, phrases, or clauses of equal grammatical rank, importance, or value.

> **Example:**   Do your duty, *or* turn in your badge.

Correlative conjunctions. Coordinating conjunctions used in pairs. Each member of the pair must be followed by words of equal grammatical value. The most common are: *either…or, neither…nor, both…and,* and *not only…but also.*

> **Example:**   *Neither* my grandfather *nor* my grandmother was born in America.

Declarative sentence. A sentence that states a fact, possibility, or condition.

Demonstrative pronoun. A pronoun pointing to, pointing out, identifying, or calling attention to: *this, that, these, those, such.*

Dependent (or subordinate) clause. A clause that does not express a complete thought in itself but which depends for its full meaning upon an independent clause in the same sentence. The three use-related classifications of dependent clauses are: *adjective, adverb,* and *noun.*

Direct object. A noun, pronoun, or noun clause following a transitive verb. (*See* **Object**.)

Direct quotation. Stating the exact words (all or part) of a writer or speaker.

Elliptical clause. An adverbial clause in which the essential parts may be omitted and implied if they refer to the same parts of the independent clause in the same sentence.

> **Example:**   *Although* [he was] *weak,* he struggled to complete the race.

Exclamatory sentence. A sentence or sentence fragment expressing strong feeling or surprise.

Future perfect tense. The time of a verb's action beginning in the present and reaching completion sometime in the future.

> **Example:**   He *will have finished* his work by this time tomorrow.

Future tense. The time of a verb expressing action or state of being after the present time.

> **Example:**   She *will be* ten years old next Tuesday.

Gender. The classification of nouns or pronouns indicating sex: *masculine, feminine, neuter, or common.*

Gerund. A verbal noun, *i.e.,* a noun formed from a verb. Gerunds end with *-ing.*

> **Example:**   *Exercising* is a great way to stay healthy both physically and mentally.

Helping verb. See *Auxiliary verb.*

Imperative mood. Used to issue a command or express a request.

Imperative sentence. A sentence expressing a command or declaring a request.

Indefinite pronoun. A pronoun with an implied antecedent but referring to no specific person, place, or thing: *one, someone, everyone, somebody, everybody, each, none, no one, nobody, everything, nothing,* etc.

Independent clause. A clause that expresses a complete thought in its context and could, if necessary, stand alone as a complete sentence.

> **Example:**   If she is chosen next Friday night, *Kim will be the first Chinese homecoming queen in the school's history.*

Indicative mood. Used to state (indicate) a fact or to ask a question of fact.

Indirect object. A noun or pronoun preceding a direct object of a verb and indicating a recipient of the object of the verb. An indirect object usually could have the prepositions *to* or *for* placed before it.

Example: I sent *Mother* a birthday card. (*I sent [to]* **Mother** *a birthday card.*)

Infinitive. A verb form that is the first principal part of a verb, equivalent to the first person present tense. The infinitive has the function of a verb (as part of the predicate) but is also a verbal or in a verbal phrase, commonly used as a noun, adjective, or adverb. As a verbal it is preceded by an introductory *to*, either expressed or implied. The infinitive may also serve as the predicate of an infinitive "clause."

Infinitive "clause." An infinitive phrase that resembles a clause. It has a so-called "assumed" subject (written in the objective case) and uses an infinitive in a predicate function.

Example: She told *him to get the keys.*

Intensive pronoun. A pronoun ending with *-self,* usually non-essential to the sentence but added for emphasis or intensification of its antecedent.

Example: I will make the announcement *myself.*

Interjection. An exclamatory word expressing strong feeling or surprise and having little or no grammatical connection with other words in a sentence.

Examples: *Ouch!* That hurts. *Oh,* what a lovely day!

Interrogative pronoun. A pronoun used in a question: *who, which, what, whoever, whatever.*

Interrogative sentence. A sentence asking a question. A question mark is used as its closing punctuation.

Intransitive verbs. Verbs that do not need an object to complete their meaning.

Examples: The music *stopped* for a moment. (*intransitive, has no object*)
He *stopped* his car. (*transitive, has an object*)

Irregular verbs. Verbs whose past and past participle forms are different in spelling from the present (infinitive) form and do not follow the regular pattern of having the last two principal parts formed by the addition of the letters *-d, -t,* or *-ed.* (*See also Appendix, page 115.*)

Examples: *see, seeing, saw, seen; drive, driving, drove, driven; lose, losing, lost, lost; set, setting, set, set*

Linking verb. A non-action verb that expresses a state of being or fixed condition. It "links" a subject to a noun or adjective (or equivalent phrase or clause) in the predicate. The most common linking verbs are forms of *be, look, seem, appear, feel, smell, sound, become, grow, remain, stand, turn, prove.*

Examples: She *is* small. His theory *proved* correct.
You *look* better today.
That dog *smells* bad.
The word of the Lord *stands* secure.

Modify. To describe or limit. Adjectives and adverbs *modify* other words.

Examples: sang *happily* (describes), the *only* child (limits)

Mood of verbs. Indicates the *state of mind* or *manner* in which a statement is made. English verbs have three moods: *indicative, imperative,* and *subjunctive.*

Nominative. The *case* of nouns or pronouns used as subjects or predicate complements.

Example: *He* is Lord. This is *he.*

Non-restrictive or **non-essential.** A modifier, usually a phrase or clause, that does not limit but describes or adds information.

Noun. A part of speech that names a person, place, thing, idea, action, or quality.

> **Examples:** *John, sky, table, capitalism, eating, godliness*

Number. The form of a noun or pronoun showing whether one or more than one is indicated. Nouns and pronouns are either *singular* (one) in number or *plural* (two or more) in number. Verbs have singular or plural forms corresponding to the number of the nouns or pronouns that perform their action or state of being.

> **Examples:** The *boy sings*. (*singular noun and verb*)
>
> The *children sing*. (*plural noun and verb*)

Object. The noun, pronoun, or noun clause following a transitive verb or preposition.

> **Examples:** Larry ate the *cake*. (*noun as object of a transitive verb*)
>
> Put the cake on the *table*. (*noun as object of a preposition*)
>
> She gave him *what he wanted*. (*noun clause as object of a transitive verb*)

Objective. The *case* of nouns or pronouns used as objects of prepositions or as direct or indirect objects of verbs.

> **Example:** I gave *him* some advice. Tell your problems to *me*. She loves *us* very much.

Participial phrase. A phrase introduced by a participle, or a participle and adverbial modifiers.

Participle. A verb form functioning either as a verb in a predicate or as an adjective. Participles have three forms: *present participle, past participle,* and *perfect participle.*

> **Examples:** I am *enjoying* my lunch. (*present participle in a predicate*)
>
> I have *finished* my lunch. (*past participle in a predicate*)
>
> A *steaming* bowl of soup would make a good lunch. (*present participle as adjective*)
>
> *Having been warned*, I bypassed the road construction. (*perfect participle used as adjective*)

Part of speech. A classification for every word in a language. In English, the primary parts of speech are: *noun, pronoun, adjective, verb, adverb, preposition, conjunction,* and *interjection.*

Passive voice. The form of a verb telling that the subject is not the doer of the action but the entity which is acted upon.

> **Example:** The song *was performed* by the choir.

Past participle. The fourth principal part of a verb used as part of a predicate or an adjective.

> **Example:** I have *eaten* my breakfast. (*fourth form of the verb **eat, eating, ate, eaten***)

Past perfect tense. The time of a verb beginning at a point in the past and ending at a later point in the past.

> **Example:** She *had said* the same thing before.

Past tense. The time of a verb before now. The third principal part of a verb.

> **Example:** She *baked* a cake. (*third form of the verb: **bake, baking, baked, [have/had] baked***)

Perfect infinitive. Formed by the auxiliary *to have* and the past participle.

> **Example:** *to have loved*

Perfect participle. Formed by the auxiliary *having* and the past participle.

> **Example:** *having loved*

Person. The form of a pronoun (and corresponding form of a verb) indicating whether the "person" or "thing" represented by the pronoun is the entity speaking or writing (*first person: I/we* worship), the entity spoken or written to (*second person*: you worship), or the entity spoken or written about (*third person*: he/she/it/they worship).

Personal pronoun. A pronoun referring to the speaker or writer, the person spoken or written to, or the person spoken or written about.

   Examples: *I, you, he, she, it, we, they, me, him, her, she, us, them*

Phrase. A group of related words not containing a subject and predicate.

   Example: The sound *of the old church bell* brought back many memories.

Plural. The classification of nouns, pronouns, subjects, and predicates indicating a number of two or more.

   Examples: *cows; they; The animals graze.*

Positive degree. The simple form of an adjective or adverb expressing no comparison.

   Examples: The *blue* sky. The *old* woman. The *beautiful* words of the psalm.

Possessive case. Used to indicate a relationship of *possession* (something that is owned).

Predicate. The verb or verb phrase in a sentence that makes a statement about the subject. A *simple predicate* is the verb or verb phrase alone. A *complete predicate* is the verb or verb phrase plus its object(s), indirect object(s), and all of their modifiers. A *compound predicate* consists of two or more verbs or verb phrases in a single sentence.

   Examples: She *wrote the letter yesterday.* ("*Wrote*" *is the simple predicate;* "*wrote the letter yester-day*" *is the complete predicate.*)
   She *sealed* the envelope and *stamped* it. (*compound predicate*)

Predicate adjective. An adjective placed in a predicate after a linking verb and used to modify the subject of a sentence or clause.

   Examples: Children are *happiest* when they know that they are *loved.*

Predicate nominative. A noun, pronoun, or equivalent clause used in a predicate after a linking verb to identify the subject.

   Examples: God is our *Father.* This is not *what it seems to be.*

Preposition. A part of speech "positioned before" a noun or pronoun showing the relationship of that noun or pronoun (object) to some other word in the sentence.

   Examples: *at* school, *under* the couch, *behind* the house, *across* the ocean

Prepositional phrase. A preposition plus its object and related words. The preposition usually precedes, but sometimes follows, its object in the phrase.

   Examples: They crawled {*through the dark and damp tunnel*} {*to the other side*} {*of the cave*}.
   What is the world coming *to?*

Present participle. The second principal part of a verb. The present participle is the *-ing* form of a verb and is used as part of a predicate or as an adjective.

   Examples: He is *working* at a local factory. (*part of predicate*)
   This is the *working* part of the engine. (*adjective*)

Present perfect tense. The time of a verb beginning in the past and ending just now or still in progress in the present.

   Example: I *have been studying* all morning.

Present tense. The time of a verb showing action or state of being now.

   Example: God *loves* me.

Principal parts. The four primary forms of verbs — *present (infinitive), present participle, past, past participle* — from which all other forms and uses (tense, mood, tone, voice) of verbs are created.

> **Examples:** *(to) love, loving, loved, (have/had) loved; (to) burst, bursting, burst, (have/had) burst; (to) swim, swimming, swam, (have/had) swum (See also Irregular verbs and Regular verbs.)*

Progressive. A verb form, sometimes referred to as *progressive tense* and sometimes referred to as *progressive tone*, expressing on-going action or state of being. The progressive tense or tone consists of an appropriate form of the auxiliary verb *to be* plus the present participle.

> **Examples:** Jody *is going* to the store.
> Bill *was playing* golf this morning.
> Darlene *will be helping* her mother clean the house.

Pronoun. A part of speech used to replace a noun, often to prevent undue repetition of a noun. Pronouns include: *I, me, you, he, him, she, her, it, they, them, who, whom, which, that,* etc. Pronouns are classified as: *personal* (he), *relative* (which), *reflexive* (she gave *herself*), *interrogative* (Who?), *demonstrative* (these), *intensive* (he *himself*), *indefinite* (all), and *reciprocal* (each other).

Reciprocal pronoun. A pronoun indicating interchange. English has only two: *each other* (interchange between two) and *one another* (interchange among more than two).

Reflexive pronoun. A pronoun ending in *-self* and referring back to the subject. It usually comes after the verb and is essential to the meaning of the sentence.

> **Example:** She told *herself* not to be afraid.

Regular verbs. The most common verbs in English, they form their past and past participle forms by adding *-d, -t,* or *-ed* to the present form.

> **Examples:** *move, moved, (have/had) moved; mean, meant, (have/had) meant; laugh, laughed, (have/had) laughed*

Relative pronoun. A pronoun connecting or *relating* an adjective clause to its antecedent. They include *who, whom, which,* and *that.*

Restrictive or **essential.** A modifier, usually a phrase or clause, that limits or identifies the word modified.

Simple sentence. A sentence containing one subject (simple or compound) and one predicate (simple or compound); tantamount to one independent clause.

> **Examples:** The weather was ideal for camping. (*one simple subject and one simple predicate*)
> Rock music is loved by some people but hated by others. (*one simple subject and one compound predicate*)

Singular. The number classification of nouns, pronouns, verbs, subjects, and predicates indicating a quantity of *one.*

> **Examples:** a *girl,* the *cowboy,* a *truck;* One *game* of tennis *makes* me tired.

Subject. The noun, pronoun, noun phrase, or noun clause about which a sentence or clause makes a statement.

1. A *simple subject* is the noun or pronoun alone.

> **Example:** The *President* of the United States spoke on television.

2. A *complete subject* consists of a simple subject and all its modifiers.

> **Example:** *The President of the United States* spoke on television.

3. A *compound subject* consists of two or more subjects in a single sentence.

> **Example:** *George Washington* and *Abraham Lincoln* are two well-known Presidents.

Subjunctive mood. Used to express a *wish, doubt, necessity, uncertainty, desire, supposition, improbable condition*, or *condition contrary to fact*.

> **Examples:** If I *were* you, I would not do that.
>
> If you *see* fit, send him one of your books.

Subordinating conjunction. A conjunction connecting a dependent clause to an independent clause.

> **Examples:** *because, that, since, if, although.* I have been lonely *since* you left.

Superlative degree. The form of an adjective or adverb comparing three or more entities. It is formed by adding *-est* to one-syllable and some two-syllable adjectives or adverbs, or by preceding an adjective or adverb of two or more syllables with the word *most*.

> **Examples:** *sharpest, loudest, heaviest, most peculiar, most unpredictable*

Tense. The time of action or state of being expressed in a verb: *present, past, future* (simple tenses), *present perfect, past perfect, future perfect* (perfect tenses). The *progressive* form of a verb is sometimes called a *tense* and sometimes a *tone* within some of the other six primary tenses.

Tone. A characteristic of verb tenses indicating *progress, emphasis*, or *simple* time.

> **Examples:** *am eating* (progressive tone), *did eat* (emphatic tone), *eat* (simple tone).

Transitive verb. A verb requiring a direct object to complete its meaning.

> **Examples:** He *died* a terrible death. (*transitive, has an object*)
>
> He *died* yesterday in his sleep. (*intransitive, has no object*)

Verb. A part of speech expressing *action* or *state of being*, or *helping* another verb complete its meaning.

> **Examples:** *construct* (action verb), *is* (state of being or linking verb), *have* built (helping verb)

Verb phrase. A group of words consisting of a verb and its helpers.

> **Examples:** *has spoken, did speak, will have been spoken*

Verbals. Verb forms used as other parts of speech: *participles, gerunds*, and *infinitives*.

Voice. The form or use of a transitive verb indicating whether its subject is the doer (*active* voice) or receiver (*passive* voice) of the verb's action.

> **Examples:** The buck *stops* here. (*active voice*)
>
> The book *was written* in the 19th century. (*passive voice*)

Index